Quoting Spurgeon

Quoting Spurgeon

Charles H. Spurgeon

Edited by
Anthony J. Ruspantini
Foreword by John F. MacArthur Jr.

Baker Books

A Division of Baker Book House Co
Grand Rapids, Michigan 49516

© 1994 by Anthony J. Ruspantini

Published by Baker Books
a division of Baker Book House Company
P.O. Box 6287, Grand Rapids, MI 49516-6287

ISBN: 0-8010-8356-7

Printed in the United States of America

Unless otherwise indicated, Scripture is from the King James Version of the Bible.

To the communion of saints—"The whole family in heaven and earth" (Ephesians 3:15)—whom I love dearly and appreciate greatly.

More specifically to my wife, Mary Anne, whom I love more dearly and am indebted to unspeakably!

Charles Haddon Spurgeon
Born June 19, 1834
Died January 31, 1892

God testifying of his gifts: and by it he being dead yet speaketh.—Hebrews 11:4

The fire he thus kindled, and turned into a beacon that shone across the seas and down through the generations, was no mere brush fire of sensationalism, but an inexhaustible blaze that glowed and burned on solid hearths and was fed by the wells of the eternal Word. Here was the miracle of a bush that "burned with fire, and [yet] was not consumed."—Helmut Thielicke

Contents

Foreword

Several years ago a friend gave me a thick sheaf of paper bound in an enormous three-ring binder. Aptly titled "Priceless Legacies of the Communion of Saints," that notebook was one of the richest collections of quotations I had ever read. A generous measure of them came from the writings of Charles Haddon Spurgeon. I devoured the entire book, then gave it a prominent place on my bookshelf. It is one of a few resources I find myself turning to regularly.

Tony Ruspantini has been collecting and cataloging quotations for years. Now he is making available for the first time in published form this invaluable anthology of Spurgeon quotations. These more than 500 selections come from 74 of Spurgeon's works. They make a fine introduction to Spurgeon's writings and provide a splendid resource for preachers, teachers, and students of Scripture.

Spurgeon, of course, is often called the Prince of Preachers. His facility with English was unsurpassed by any other preacher of his age or since. He was a skillful and persuasive speaker, always fresh and challenging. Ministering to enormous crowds in the days before public address systems, Spurgeon could captivate thousands for hours at a time. But those things alone do not really explain the man's greatness.

His passion for truth was what set Spurgeon apart from others. Never one to compromise or soft-sell truth, Spurgeon forcefully declared and defended his biblical convictions. His popularity in our age belies the clouds of controversy that enveloped his ministry during his lifetime. Although today Spurgeon is almost universally admired and honored, the ironic truth is that during his lifetime he was often castigated—even despised—for his unyielding stance on crucial matters of biblical principle. His willingness to stand firm in the face of such hostility is the key to Spurgeon's real greatness.

Spurgeon's extraordinary gift of preaching as well as his unbending commitment to biblical truth shine clearly in this marvelous collection of quotations. Christians everywhere owe a debt of gratitude to Tony Ruspantini for making them available in this format.

John F. MacArthur Jr.
February 1992

Introduction

In this the one hundredth year after his death, a time in which the gospel is diluted and compromised at every turn, I sometimes wonder if it is even remotely possible to praise God enough for that incredibly marvelous gift to His Church, Charles Spurgeon! How desperately the church today needs a massive dose of Spurgeon's strong doctrinal influence!

I will thank God eternally for having been introduced to Spurgeon back in 1970, my very first year as a Christian. Having read such books as *The Soul Winner, Lectures to My Students, All of Grace,* and at least tasting the monumental *Treasury of David* during this time, I very early began jotting down some of Spurgeon's quotes in the front of my Bible for ready reference. In one of those quotes, Spurgeon says, "Oh, let us long to be used, pray to be used, and pine to be used!"[1] My earnest prayer and longing desire is that this book of Spurgeon's quotes will be used only for Christ's glory and the upbuilding of His people!

An ever-growing realization that Charles Spurgeon was in a class by himself regarding doctrinal purity, volume of works in print, and, in my sincere opinion, the most "Classic Work" in many different areas of Christian literature, has never stopped growing in the last twenty-two years in reading something over 580 Christian books by approximately two hundred authors. The above-mentioned titles would be a good illustration in four areas. Add to them his tremendous autobiography, his 700-plus page devotional, *Morning and Evening,* and his massive and marvelous *Metropolitan Tabernacle Pulpit,* and it becomes beyond impressive.

Being at present age fifty-seven myself, and realizing that Charles Spurgeon died on January 31, 1892, at the age of fifty-seven, not only humbles me to the dust, but more importantly gives me reason to love him incredibly and praise God endlessly for this precious man of God. Regarding those who are simply men, only my love for the apostle Paul rivals my sincere love and affection for Charles Spurgeon!

The Bible commands us not only to pray fervently, but without ceasing (James 5:16 and 1 Thessalonians 5:17). One of the most sobering quotations I have ever run across was by Spurgeon on James 5:16: "Supplication, in which a man's proper self is not thoroughly present in agonizing earnestness and vehement desire, is utterly ineffectual."[2] In light of some of my following comments, please let me frankly confess that I am often convicted of *my lack,* especially in the area of continual, fervent, intercessory prayer. Though it is my heart's desire to be vastly more diligent in this type of praying, I find that so very often I would rather rest than wrestle in prayer. How the apostle Paul shames me when I meditate on Colossians 1:29 and 2:1, where Paul downright agonizes in prayer over people he has not so much as even seen face to face!

I truly believe no man since Paul can take a Christian by the hand, so to speak, and teach him or her to pray the Word and principles of the Word like Charles Spurgeon. Another Spurgeon quote in the front of my first Bible reads, "Mention your own experience and plead with others to come and taste the same."[3] I can honestly say regarding Appendix B, which contains mostly shortened, paraphrased prayers, at least 50 percent of which are Spurgeon's (out of over a dozen preachers quoted), that I have spent in the vicinity of a thousand hours—and still counting—memorizing, retaining, and praying them in private. The blessing to my heart has been boundless!

The preeminent importance of being saturated with Scripture is the primary objective[4] I have been striving so hard to communicate. On that basis, it thrills my heart to interject three tremendous and pertinent Spurgeon quotations I ran across within a week of the initial writing of this introduction:

1. "I would rather lay my soul asoak in half a dozen verses all day than I would, as it were, rinse my hand in several chapters. Oh, to bathe in a text of Scripture till it saturates your heart! . . . Set your heart upon God's Word! It is the only way to know it thoroughly: let your whole nature be plunged into it as cloth into a dye."[5]

2. "In proportion as your mind becomes saturated with Holy Scripture, you are conscious of being lifted right up, and carried aloft as on eagles' wings."[6]

3. "Oh, that we might know the Spirit of Holy Scripture

thoroughly, drinking it in, till we are saturated with it! This is the blessing which we resolve to obtain."[7]

In light of these marvelous quotes, and verses such as Colossians 3:16 and Ephesians 6:17, where we are not only commanded to let the Word of Christ dwell in us richly, but to be able to take the Word of God as a sword to be used in *spiritual warfare,* in *temptation* as Christ did in Matthew 4:4 and following, in *prayer,* in *witnessing,* and in *exhorting* fellow believers, as Hebrews 3:13 commands—O fellow Christian, isn't it regarding this very point—lack of saturation in God's Word—that present day Christianity suffers its most glaring weakness?

My heart's burning desire and prayer to God is that many, many others will join me in praying prayers such as are found in Appendix B, as well as praying many areas of Scripture such as John 17, Ephesians 1:15–23, Ephesians 3:14–21, Philippians 1:8–11, Colossians 1:9–13, and Psalm 119. I have found myself praying the first six words[8] of Psalm 119:20 off and on for hours: "My soul breaketh for the longing . . ." for the sick, the dying, the lost, the lonely, those in pain, those overwhelmed by fear or depression, and even despair! I believe I can quite safely promise that those who respond to this plea (assuming it is not yet their practice) will realize a sense of the love and presence of Christ beyond the power of words to express! Psalm 39:3 says, "While I was musing, the fire burned." Jeremiah 15:16 reads, "Thy words were found, and I did eat them; and Thy word was unto me the joy and rejoicing of mine heart." In both cases it was after long meditation on God's Word that joy and rejoicing of heart resulted! According to my study, Jeremiah was going through deep, deep waters of affliction when he penned these words.

At this point, please let me say that the love and appreciation I have for my wife can be best expressed by Appendix D, where Alexander Maclaren tells what his wife meant to him and his ministry. By all means, though, please let me make it clear that neither my loving wife nor I have anything approaching the massive intellect possessed by Maclaren and his wife.

Finally, these Spurgeon quotes represent a little less than 25 percent of a collection of quotations under the unpublished work entitled "Priceless Legacies of the Communion of Saints," involving well over 2,200 quotes, covering 200-plus topics by some 150 authors, taken from over 300 sources. This initial compilation just would not have even begun without the tremendous encouragement and editorial advice of Phil Johnson and Dr. John MacArthur. My eternal debt and gratitude to them both is incalculable!

Anthony J. Ruspantini

Adoration

Trust is one of the sublimest forms of *adoration*.

C. H. Spurgeon, *Metropolitan Tabernacle Pulpit*, Vol. 33,
p. 466 [Ephesians 1:12–13]

Affections

Certainly, the benefit of reading must come to the soul by the way of the understanding. When the high priest went into the holy place he always lit the golden candlestick before he kindled the incense upon the brazen altar, as if to show that the mind must have illumination before the *affections* can properly rise towards their divine object. There must be knowledge of God before there can be *love* to God: there must be a knowledge of divine things, as they are revealed, before there can be an enjoyment of them.

C. H. Spurgeon, *Words of Counsel for Christian Workers*, p. 108
[Psalm 39:3]

Blessedness is ascribed to those who treasure up the testimonies of the Lord. . . . We must first get a thing before we can keep it. In order to keep it well we must get a firm grip on it: we cannot keep in the heart that which we have not heartily embraced by the *affections*.

C. H. Spurgeon, *The Treasury of David*, Vol. 3, Pt. 1, p. 141
[Psalm 119:2, 11, 16]

17

Affliction

Rutherford had a quaint saying, that when he was cast into the cellars of *affliction,* he remembered that the great King always kept His wine there.

> C. H. Spurgeon, *C. H. Spurgeon's Prayers,* p. 154 [Jeremiah 33:3]

Faith always sees the bow of the covenant promise whenever sense sees the cloud of *affliction.*

> C. H. Spurgeon, *Faith's Checkbook,* p. 6 [Genesis 9:14]

Patience is a pearl which is only found in the deep seas of *affliction;* and only grace can find it there, bring it to the surface, and adorn the neck of faith therewith.

> C. H. Spurgeon, *Metropolitan Tabernacle Pulpit,* Vol. 32, p. 314

Agony, Agonizing

Supplication, in which a man's proper self is not thoroughly present in *agonizing* earnestness and vehement desire, is utterly ineffectual.

> C. H. Spurgeon, *Morning and Evening,* p. 31 [Psalm 109:4; James 5:16]

Silent prayers are often true prayers, but there are times, in extremity of suffering, it is very helpful to give expression to the soul's *agony.* . . . The use of the voice . . . gives intensity to the desires.

> C. H. Spurgeon, *Spurgeon's Expository Encyclopedia,* Vol. 15, p. 279 [Psalm 142:1]

Alone

Secret religion is the very soul of godliness. What we are *alone,* that *alone* we are. Private communion with Jesus is a better sign of grace than all the outward sacraments that were ever attended. It is not likely that a hypocrite will delight in solitary devotion; there is nothing in it to pay him for his trouble; for his reward is the praise of man. Judgment upon ourselves will be much more likely to be correct, if we examine our hidden life than if we measure ourselves by that which is seen of men.

C. H. Spurgeon, *Flowers From a Puritan's Garden*, p. 172

Amen

Amen has four meanings in Scripture. . . . "Lord, let it be so"—it is the heart's desire. . . . It means the affirmation of our faith. . . . It often expresses the joy of the heart. . . . It means, "I, in the name of God, solemnly pledge myself that in His strength I will seek to make it so; to Him be glory both now and for ever."

C. H. Spurgeon, *The Treasury of the Bible*, Vol. 8, pp. 472–473
[2 Peter 3:18]

Audible Prayer

Silent prayers are often true prayers, but there are times, in extremity of suffering, it is very helpful to *give expression* to the soul's agony. I know some friends who can never pray to their own comfort except they can *hear their own voices;* and I believe that it is a good thing for the most of us to retire to some private place where we cannot be heard by men, and where we can therefore freely *use our voices* in prayer. Very often, the use of the voice helps to keep the thoughts from wandering, and also gives intensity to the desires. You notice that David particularly mentions here that he *cried* unto the Lord *with his voice.* No doubt many of his prayers ascended to God from his heart without the medium of *his voice;* but here, the *cry with voice* went with the desires of his heart.

C. H. Spurgeon, *Spurgeon's Expository Encyclopedia*, Vol. 15,
p. 279 [Psalm 142:1]

Behold

A sight of Jesus by faith is the pleasure of *beholding* Him in His glory and being transformed into His image.

C. H. Spurgeon, *Faith's Checkbook*, p. 67 [2 Corinthians 3:18]

The glory of the divine Trinity overawes us until we *behold* the milder radiance of the Incarnate God.

C. H. Spurgeon, *According to Promise*, p. 125 [2 Corinthians 1:20]

In a word, by faith we *behold* the glory of the Lord as in a glass, and we are changed into the same image—and the image of God is love.

C. H. Spurgeon, *Complete in Christ and Love's Logic*, p. 106

O, my blessed Master, help me I pray Thee to keep the mirror of my mind in the right position, that evermore I may *see* Thee. True, it will be but as in a glass darkly, but even that will be a marvelous preparation for *beholding* Thee face to face.

C. H. Spurgeon, *Flowers From a Puritan's Garden*, p. 268

O Lord . . . Let us *gaze* upon Thy glory till we are transformed by the sight, and become Christ-like among the sons of men.

C. H. Spurgeon, *C. H. Spurgeon's Prayers*, p. 76

O Lord God, help us now really to worship Thee. . . . Enable us to rise clean out of this world. May we get rid of all its down-dragging tendencies. May the attractions of these grosser things be gone, and do Thou catch us away to Thyself. We do not ask to be entranced nor to see an angel in shining apparel, but we do ask that by faith we may *see* Jesus, and may His presence be so evidently realized among us that we may rejoice as well as if our eyes *beheld* Him.

> C. H. Spurgeon, *C. H. Spurgeon's Prayers*, p. 7 [Hebrews 12:2; 3:1]

Why, if this Book said no more than "they shall be with me where I am, that they may *behold* My glory," we should know enough of heaven to make our hearts dance for joy. To be with Jesus where He is, to *behold* His glory, this is bliss pressed down and running over, more than our bosoms can hold.

> C. H. Spurgeon, *The Treasury of the Bible*, Vol. 3, p. 55 [Psalm 119:54]

Bliss

What a heaven of *bliss* lies slumbering in those three words, "I am thine."

> C. H. Spurgeon, *Spurgeon's Expository Encyclopedia*, Vol. 15, p. 264 [Psalm 119:94]

My witness is, that those who are honoured of their Lord in public have usually to endure a secret chastening, or carry a peculiar cross, lest by any means they exalt themselves, and fall into the snare of the devil. Glory to God for the furnace, the hammer, and the file. Heaven shall be all the fuller of *bliss* because we have been filled with anguish here below, and earth shall be better tilled because of our training in the school of adversity.

> C. H. Spurgeon, *Lectures to My Students*, p. 164

Boanerges

We must sound an alarm; we should be traitors to men's souls and to our Master if we always piped to dulcet music. He who is always comforting his people will find no comfort when he is called to answer for it before his God another day. Many souls need *Boanerges* more than Barnabas, *thunder* more than dew. By many who think themselves great judges the trumpet discourse is judged to be too harsh, and the piper is commended for his pleasant strains; and yet the Lord may distribute the praise and the blame very differently.

My heart, be not thou always craving for soft music. Be willing to be startled and stimulated. Life is a conflict, and thou needest battle music to keep thee up to fighting pitch. Let those who dance with the world pay the pipers who play to them; as for thee, give thine ear to the King's trumpeters.

C. H. Spurgeon, *Flowers From a Puritan's Garden*, pp. 58–59

Books

Use all means and helps towards the understanding of the Scriptures. When Philip asked the Ethiopian eunuch whether he understood the prophecy of Isaiah he replied, "How can I, unless some man should guide me?" . . . Some under the pretence of being taught of the Spirit of God, refuse to be instructed by *books* or by living men. This is no honouring of the Spirit of God; it is a disrespect to Him, for if He gives to some of His servants more light than to others—and it is clear He does—then they are bound to give that light to others, and to use it for the good of the church. But if the other part of the church refuse to receive that light, to what end did the Spirit of God give it? This would imply that there is a mistake somewhere in the economy of gifts and graces, which is managed by the Holy Spirit. . . .

22

It would be most wicked of us to say, "We will not have the heavenly treasure which exists in earthen vessels."

> C. H. Spurgeon, *Words of Counsel for Christian Workers,*
> pp. 112–113

Both Paul and Tyndale requested *books* as their companions as they awaited trial and certain death. Charles Spurgeon had a marvelous comment on Paul's request:

"He is inspired, yet he wants *books!* He has been preaching at least for 30 years, yet he wants *books!* He has seen the Lord, and yet he wants *books!* He has had a wider experience than most men, yet he wants *books!* He had been caught up into the third heaven, and had heard things which it is unlawful for a man to utter, yet he wants *books!* He had written the major part of the New Testament, yet he wants *books!*"

How I wish that this same desire for *good books* characterized more believers today!

> *Victorious Christians You Should Know,* p. 8 [2 Timothy 4:13]

Bread of Life

Faith gathers the handfuls of sacred corn from which contemplation threshes out the ears and prepares soul-sustaining *bread.*

> C. H. Spurgeon, *The Best of C. H. Spurgeon,* p. 38

Camp

The church is spiritually a *camp.* . . . It is a *camp* for separation. . . . The great object of a Christian should be to separate the church more and more entirely from the world.

> C. H. Spurgeon, *Spurgeon's Expository Encyclopedia,* Vol. 15,
> p. 137 [Deuteronomy 23:14]

Multitudes are for ever playing at being Christians. Do you note their childish see-saw, up and down, up and down;

but their movement leaves them no higher than at first. God save us from this! The *camp* must go onward. Thus saith the Lord, "Speak unto the children of Israel, that they go forward." We ought to be advancing in grace, in knowledge, in earnestness, in holiness, in usefulness, and if not, we scarcely realize the figure of a *camp*.

> C. H. Spurgeon, *Spurgeon's Expository Encyclopedia*, Vol. 15, p. 140 [Deuteronomy 23:14]

A *camp* of angels should not be more holy than a church of saints among whom the Lord God hath taken up His abode.

> C. H. Spurgeon, *Spurgeon's Expository Encyclopedia*, Vol. 15, p. 141 [Deuteronomy 23:14]

"The Lord thy God is a jealous God." See, then, the argument: if it be so, that God is specially watchful over His church, let thy *camp* be holy.

> C. H. Spurgeon, *Spurgeon's Expository Encyclopedia*, Vol. 15, p. 142 [Deuteronomy 6:15; 23:14]

If we do not meet again in this wilderness below, may we meet, when *camp* life is over, in the city above, to go no more out forever! The blessing of the Lord rest on you evermore!

> C. H. Spurgeon, *Spurgeon's Expository Encyclopedia*, Vol. 15, p. 146 [Deuteronomy 23:14]

Care, Careful

That religion which needs no *care*, and takes no trouble, is in great demand in the world; it is produced by the acre, and may be spread over the surface everywhere. Not so the religion of grace; it costs many a tear, and a world of anxious thought, and solemn heart-searching, and it is but slow work at the best; but then it is of great price, and is not only acceptable with God, but even men perceive that there is something about it to which the common religious daubers never attain.

C. H. Spurgeon, *Flowers From a Puritan's Garden*, p. 47

If we let the boat drift with the stream, and leave our religion to random influences, without *care* or thought, what can we look for but slovenliness and worthlessness? If we would please God we must watch every stroke and touch upon the canvas of our lives, and we may not think that we can lay it on with a trowel and yet succeed.

C. H. Spurgeon, *Flowers From a Puritan's Garden*, p. 47

We ought to live as miniature-painters work, for they watch every line and tint. O for more *careful work*, more heart work!

C. H. Spurgeon, *Flowers From a Puritan's Garden*, p. 47

Charles Spurgeon

Sometimes we have seen a model marriage, founded on pure love, and cemented in mutual esteem. Therein, the husband acts as a tender head; and the wife, as a true spouse, realizes the model marriage-relation, and sets forth what our oneness with the Lord ought to be. She delights in her husband, in his person, his character, his affection; to her, he is not only the chief and foremost of mankind, but in her eyes he is all-in-all; her heart's love belongs to him, and to him only. She finds sweetest content and solace in his company, his fellowship, his fondness; he is her little world, her Paradise, her choice treasure. At any time, she would gladly lay aside her own pleasure to find it doubled in gratifying him. She is glad to sink her individuality in his. She seeks no renown for herself; his honour is reflected upon her, and she rejoices in it. She would defend his name with her dying breath; safe enough is he where she can speak for him. The domestic circle is her kingdom; that she may there create happiness and comfort, is her life-work; and his smiling gratitude is all the reward she seeks. Even in her dress, she thinks of him; without constraint she consults his taste, and considers nothing beautiful which is distasteful to him. A tear from his eye, because of any unkindness on her part would grievously torment her. She asks not how her behaviour may please a stranger, or how another's judgment may approve her conduct; let her beloved be content, and she is glad. He has many objects in life, some of which she does not quite understand; but she believes in them all, and anything that she can do to promote them, she delights to perform. He lavishes love on her, and, in return, she lavishes love on him. Their object in life is common. There are points where their affections so intimately unite that none could tell which is first and which is second. . . .

Happy woman and happy man! If heaven be found on earth, they have it! At last, the two are so blended, so engrafted on one stem, that their old age presents a lovely attachment, a common sympathy, by which its infirmities are greatly alleviated, and its burdens are transformed into fresh bonds of love. So happy a union of will, sentiment, thought, and heart exists between them, that the two streams of their life have washed away the dividing bank, and run on as one broad current of united existence till their common joy falls into the ocean of eternal felicity.

C. H. Spurgeon, *C. H. Spurgeon Autobiography,* Vol. 1, "The Early Years," p. 410

It was ever the settled purpose of my married life that I should never hinder him *[Charles Spurgeon]* in his work for the Lord, never try to keep him from fulfilling his engagements, never plead my own ill-health as a reason why he should remain at home with me. I thank God, now, that He enabled me to carry out this determination, and rejoice that I have no cause to reproach myself with being a drag on the swift wheels of his consecrated life.

Mrs. C. H. Spurgeon, *C. H. Spurgeon Autobiography,* Vol. 1,
"The Early Years," p. 289

No matter what words one may speak with eloquence of tongue or write with skill of pen, a woeful sense of inadequacy would oppress orator and writer in making an effort to express the worth and wonder of *Charles Haddon Spurgeon's* sermons. Veritable beds of Gospel pearls are all the sermons of this remarkable preacher so greatly used of God. . . . A sense of inadequacy is upon me as I speak of *Charles Haddon Spurgeon* and his sermons. No eloquence of tongue nor skill of pen can fully describe the man and his message. . . . In his preaching this giant of God flowed as a river and never did trickle as a rill. By lip and life he shone as a chandelier—never as a flickering candle. The man and his message made a scriptural orchestra of many instruments. He was a great organ whose full breath was thunder beneath God's fingers pressed.

Robert G. Lee, *Spurgeon's Sermons Preached on Unusual
Occasions,* p. 270

The mightiest of the mighty and the noblest of the noble! When it comes to pulpiteers, truly these words describe only one man: *Charles Haddon Spurgeon.*

I have read the sermons of *Charles Spurgeon* with greater profit than those of any other man, living or dead. The careful perusal of their structure and content has been more helpful than all of my seminary courses in homiletics combined.

In every art form students have learned their craft by studying the works of the masters. Outside the pages of Holy Writ, it is without controversy that for sustained and unparalleled sermon production, *Charles Spurgeon* is the preacher par excellence. To occupy the pulpit and to fail to study carefully such a master of the art as this, can only result in great loss to ourselves and our congregations. Soli Deo Gloria.

> D. James Kennedy, *An Introduction to the Life and Ministry of Charles Haddon Spurgeon*, p. 40 (Compiled by Bob L. Ross)

When I get to Heaven, after I see the Saviour and my own dear family, I want to see Charles Haddon Spurgeon. To me he is the greatest preacher who has ever lived.

The Apostle Paul wrote the inspired word. *Spurgeon* interprets it in all its rich meaning to my heart.

> W. A. Criswell, *Spurgeon's Sermons Preached on Unusual Occasions*, p. 260

Child, Children

You do not thoroughly know any truth till you can put it before a *child* so that he can see it.

> C. H. Spurgeon, *Come Ye Children*, p. 73 [Psalm 34:11]

A *child* is usually far less reticent than a man; the little lip is not frozen by cold prudence, but reveals the heart.

> C. H. Spurgeon, *Come Ye Children*, p. 140

Youthful piety is a very touching thing to me; I see the grace of God in men and women with much thankfulness, but I cannot perceive it in *children* without shedding tears of delight. There is an exceeding beauty about these rosebuds of the Lord's garden; they have a fragrance which we find not in the fairest of earth's lilies. Love is won for the Lord Jesus in many a heart by these tiny arrows of the Lord, whose very smallness is a part of the power to penetrate the heart.

> C. H. Spurgeon, *Come Ye Children*, pp. 137–138

Christ

Christ chose this weapon [the Word] out of all the others, and used it in His earliest conflict, so too, He used it when no man was near. The value of Holy Scripture is not alone seen in public teaching or striving for the truth; its still small voice is equally powerful when the servant of the Lord is enduring personal trial in the lone wilderness.

C.H. Spurgeon, *Spurgeon's Expository Encyclopedia*, Vol. 15, p. 322 [Matthew 4:4; Ephesians 6:17]

Church

Lord, restore to Thy *Church* the love of strong doctrine. May Thy truth yet prevail. Purge out from among Thy *Church* those who would lead others away from the truth. . . . May we live to see Thy *Church* shine forth clear as the sun and fair as the moon, and terrible as an army with banners.

C. H. Spurgeon, *C. H. Spurgeon's Prayers*, p. 82

We want *churches* that know the truth, and are well taught in the things of God. If we taught better they would learn better. See how little many professors know; not enough to give them discernment between living truth and deadly error. Old-fashioned believers could give you chapter and verse for what they believed; but how few of such remain! To try to shake them was by no means a hopeful task: you might as well have hoped to shake the pillars of the universe; for they were steadfast, and could not be carried about with every wind of doctrine. They knew what they knew, and they held fast that which they had learned. Oh, for a *church* of out-and-out believers, impervious to the soul-destroying doubt which pours upon us in showers!

The Greatest Fight in the World, C. H. Spurgeon's "Final Manifesto," pp. 45–46 [Ephesians 4:14; Romans 6:17]

In proportion as we have more regard for the sacred Godhead, the wondrous Trinity in Unity, shall we see a greater display of God's power and a more glorious manifestation of His might in our *churches.*

C. H. Spurgeon, *Metropolitan Tabernacle Pulpit,* Vol. 1, p. 379

Churchgoers

I believe a very large majority of *churchgoers* are merely unthinking, slumbering worshipers of an unknown God.

C. H. Spurgeon, *Metropolitan Tabernacle Pulpit,* Vol. 11, p. 496 [1 Peter 1:16; Matthew 5:6, 8]

Clarity

What marvel if, under some men's shifty talk, people grow into love of both truth and falsehood! The fact is, they would like anything if only a clever deceiver would put it plausibly before them. They admire Moses and Aaron, but they would not say a word against Jannes and Jambres. We shall not join in the confederacy which seems to aim at such a comprehension. We must preach the gospel so *distinctly* that our people know what we are preaching. "If the trumpet give an uncertain sound, who shall prepare himself for the battle?" We shall not hesitate to speak in the strongest Saxon words we can find, and in the plainest sentences we can put together, that which we hold as fundamental truth.

The Greatest Fight in the World, C. H. Spurgeon's "Final Manifesto," pp. 38–39 [1 Corinthians 14:8]

If there be living water in your preaching, it may be very deep, but the light of truth will give *clearness* to it.

C. H. Spurgeon, *Lectures to My Students,* p. 210

Comfort (Consolation)

Great hearts can only be made by great troubles. The spade of trouble digs the reservoir of *comfort* deeper, and makes more room for *consolation.*

> C. H. Spurgeon, *Words of Cheer for Daily Life*, p. 24
> [2 Corinthians 1:3–5]

A ploughman . . . said to me, "Depend upon it, if you or I ever get one inch above the ground, we shall get just that inch too high." I believe it is true; for the lower we lie, the nearer to the ground we are—the more our troubles humble us—the more fit we are to receive *comfort;* and God always gives us *comfort* when we are most fit for it.

> C. H. Spurgeon, *Words of Cheer for Daily Life*, p. 24
> [2 Corinthians 1:3–5]

Consolations increase in the same ratio as our trials.

> C. H. Spurgeon, *Words of Cheer for Daily Life*, p. 24
> [2 Corinthians 1:3–5]

Where showers fall most, there the grass is greenest. I suppose the fogs and mists of Ireland make it "the Emerald Isle"; and wherever you find great fogs of trouble, and mists of sorrow, you always find emerald green hearts: full of the beautiful verdure of the *comfort* and love of God.

> C. H. Spurgeon, *Words of Cheer for Daily Life*, pp. 24–25
> [2 Corinthians 1:3–5]

Compromise

We should guard ourselves against *compromising* the truth of God by association with those who do not hold it, especially at such a time as this.

> C. H. Spurgeon, *Spurgeon's Sermons Preached on Unusual Occasions*, p. 216

What marvel if, under some men's shifty talk, people grow into love of *both truth and falsehood!* The fact is, they would like anything if only a clever deceiver would put it plausibly before them. They admire Moses and Aaron, but they would not say a word against Jannes and Jambres. We shall not join in the confederacy which seems to aim at such a comprehension. We must preach the gospel so distinctly that our people know what we are preaching. "If the trumpet give an uncertain sound, who shall prepare himself for the battle?" We shall not hesitate to speak in the strongest Saxon words we can find, and in the plainest sentences we can put together, that which we hold as fundamental truth.

> *The Greatest Fight in the World,* C. H. Spurgeon's "Final Manifesto," pp. 38–39

Condescension

I bow with reverent amazement, my heart sinking into the dust with adoration, when I reflect that God the Holy Ghost helps us when we cannot speak, but only groan. Yes, and when we cannot even utter our groanings, He doth not only help us but He claims as His own particular creation the "groanings that cannot be uttered." This is *condescension* indeed!

> C. H. Spurgeon, *Metropolitan Tabernacle Pulpit,* Vol. 26, p. 228 [Romans 8:26–27; Psalm 38:9]

Conformed to Christ

Regarding the word "will" in John 17:24, Spurgeon says it means, "a deliberate desire—a forcible, distinct, resolute, determined purpose."

> *Metropolitan Tabernacle Pulpit,* Vol. 32, p. 174

[Compiler's comment: O fellow believer, especially you who are privileged to preach or teach the Word, if you have not done so already, please put John 17:24 alongside 2 Corinthians 3:18—Amplified Bible, and see if it doesn't almost preach of itself one of the most beautiful sermons that can be imagined! I believe with all my heart that this is the basic message that the greatest preachers of all time have preached to countless generations! "Let the word of Christ dwell in you richly" (Colossians 3:16) would be the practical application simply stated.]

The prayerful study of the Word is not only a means of instruction, but an act of devotion wherein the *transforming* power of grace is often exercised, *changing* us into the image of Him of whom the Word is a mirror.

> *The Greatest Fight in the World,* C. H. Spurgeon's "Final Manifesto," p. 20 [John 17:24; 2 Corinthians 3:18; Colossians 3:16]

Death . . . comes to us as a covenant blessing *conforming* us to Christ.

> C. H. Spurgeon, *The Treasury of the Bible,* Vol. 3, p. 18 [Psalm 116:15]

Faith is an act of the understanding; but it also proceeds from the heart. God gives salvation to faith because it resides next door to the affections, and is near akin to love; and love is the parent and the nurse of every holy feeling and act. Love to God is obedience, love to God is holiness. To love God and to love man is to be *conformed to the image of Christ;* and this is salvation.

> C. H. Spurgeon, *All of Grace,* p. 62 [Romans 10:9; John 14:21]

In a word, by faith we behold the glory of the Lord as in a glass, and we are *changed into the same image*—and the image of God is love.

> C. H. Spurgeon, *Complete in Christ and Love's Logic,* p. 106

Death

The *departures* of the saints cause us many a pang. . . . Be it known that while we are sorrowing Christ is rejoicing. His prayer is, "Father, I will that they also whom Thou hast given Me be with Me where I am."

> C. H. Spurgeon, *The Treasury of the Bible*, Vol. 3, p. 17 [Psalm 116:15; John 17:24]

Faith . . . muzzles the mouth of *death*.

> C. H. Spurgeon, *Spurgeon's Expository Encyclopedia*, Vol. 15, p. 92 [Hebrews 11:5]

Death . . . comes to us as a covenant blessing conforming us to Christ.

> C. H. Spurgeon, *The Treasury of the Bible*, Vol. 3, p. 18 [Psalm 116:15]

If I might make my choice between living till Christ comes, so as to be changed only, and not to *die*, or of actually sleeping in the dust, I would prefer to *die*, for in this the believer who shall *fall asleep* will be the more closely conformed to Christ Jesus.

> C. H. Spurgeon, *The Treasury of the Bible*, Vol. 3, p. 18 [Psalm 116:15]

Delay

Love presides over the arrangements of grace and strikes upon the bell when the best moment has arrived. God blesses us by His *temporary delays*, as well as by His prompt replies.

> C. H. Spurgeon, *According to Promise*, p. 116 [Acts 7:17; John 11:5–6]

Love closes the hand of divine bounty, and *restrains* the outflow of favour, when it sees that a solid gain will ensue from a period of trial. . . . The time of the promise corresponds with the time most enriching to heart and soul.

C. H. Spurgeon, *According to Promise*, pp. 116–117 [Acts 7:17; John 11:5–6]

Delay has produced the patience of hope, and made every mercy to wear a double value.

C. H. Spurgeon, *According to Promise*, p. 57

Frequently the richest answers are not the speediest. . . . A prayer may be all the longer on its voyage because it is bringing us a heavier freight of blessing. *Delayed* answers are not only trials of faith, but they give us an opportunity of honouring God by our steadfast confidence in Him under apparent repulses.

C. H. Spurgeon, *Flowers From a Puritan's Garden*, p. 266 [Habakkuk 2:3]

Delight

Holy David makes *delight* such an ingredient or assistant here, that sometimes he calls the exercise of meditation by the name of "delight," speaking in the foregoing verse of this meditation.

C. H. Spurgeon (quoting Nathanael Ranew), *The Treasury of David*, Vol. 3, Pt. 1, p. 161 [Psalm 119:16]

"I will *delight* myself in thy statutes." In this verse *delight* follows meditation, of which it is the true flower and outgrowth. When we have no other solace, but are quite alone, it will be a glad thing for the heart to turn upon itself, and sweetly whisper, "I will *delight* myself. What if no minstrel sings in the hall, I will *delight* myself. If the time of the singing of birds has not yet arrived, and the voice of the turtle is not heard in our land, yet I will *delight* myself." This is the choicest and noblest of all rejoicing; in fact, it is the good part which can never be taken from us; but there is no *delighting* ourselves with anything below that which God intended to be the soul's eternal satisfaction. . . . When the believer once peruses the sacred pages his soul burns within him as he turns first to one and then to another of the royal words of the great King, words full and firm, immutable and divine.

> C. H. Spurgeon, *The Treasury of David*, Vol. 3, Pt. 1, p. 161
> [Psalm 119:16; Jeremiah 15:16]

This is the true art of memory, to cause them to *delight* in what they learn. Such instructions as we take in with sweetness, they stick with us, and run in our minds night and day.

> C. H. Spurgeon (quoting Thomas Manton), *The Treasury of David*, Vol. 3, Pt. 1, p. 161 [Psalm 119:16]

"*Delight* myself." The word is very emphatical . . . I will skip about and jump for *joy*.

> C. H. Spurgeon (quoting Adam Clarke), *The Treasury of David*, Vol. 3, Pt. 1, p. 161 [Psalm 119:16]

Depression

Although my joy is greater than most men, my *depression* is such as few have an idea of.

> C. H. Spurgeon, *Metropolitan Tabernacle Pulpit*, Vol. 14, p. 188

I often feel very grateful to God that I have undergone fearful *depression*. I know the borders of despair and the horrible brink of that gulf of darkness into which my feet have almost gone. But hundreds of times I have been able to give a helpful grip to brethren and sisters who have come into the same condition. . . . I believe that the darkest and most dreadful experience of a child of God will help him to be a fisher of men if he will but follow Christ.

> C. H. Spurgeon, *Metropolitan Tabernacle Pulpit*, Vol. 32, p. 344

As it is recorded that David, in the heat of battle, waxed faint, so it may be written of all of the servants of the Lord. Fits of *depression* come over the most of us.

C. H. Spurgeon, *Lectures to My Students*, p. 154

The life of Luther might suffice to give a thousand instances, and he was by no means of the weaker sort. His great spirit was often in seventh heaven of exultation, and as frequently on the borders of *despair.*

C. H. Spurgeon, *Lectures to My Students*, p. 154

My witness is, that those who are honoured of their Lord in public have usually to endure a secret chastening, or carry a peculiar cross, lest by any means they exalt themselves, and fall into the snare of the devil. Glory to God for the furnace, the hammer, and the file. Heaven shall be all the fuller of bliss because we have been filled with *anguish* here below, and earth shall be better tilled because of our training in the school of adversity.

C. H. Spurgeon, *Lectures to My Students*, p. 164

Lord, end my winter, and let my spring begin. I cannot with all my longing raise my soul out of her *death and dulness,* but all things are possible with Thee. I need celestial influences, the clear shinings of Thy love, the beams of Thy grace, the light of Thy countenance, these are the Pleiades to me. I suffer much from sin and temptation, these are my wintry signs, my terrible Orion. Lord, work wonders in me, and for me.

C. H. Spurgeon, *Morning and Evening*, p. 163 [Job 38:31]

All *depressing* circumstances lose their power for evil when our faith takes firm hold upon the promises of God.

C. H. Spurgeon, *According to Promise*, p. 67

There is a quiet, rippling rill of intense comfort in a Christian's heart, even when he is *cast down* and tried, and at other times when trials are lightened there are cascades of delight, leaping cataracts of joy, whose silver spray is as pure as the flash of the fountains of Paradise. I know that there are many here who, like myself, understand what deep *depression* of spirit means, but yet we would not change our lot for all the mirth of fools or pomp of kings. . . . Amid the ashes of our pains live the sparks of our joys, ready to flame up when the breath of the Spirit sweetly blows thereon. Our latent happiness is a choicer heritage than the sinner's riotous glee.

> C. H. Spurgeon, *The Treasury of the Bible*, Vol. 3, p. 53 [Psalm 119:54; John 17:24]

Desire (Longing, Intensity, Earnestness)

A groan cometh not from the lips, but from the heart. A groan then is a part of prayer which we owe to the Holy Ghost, and the same is true of all the prayer which wells up from the deep fountains of our inner life. The prophet cried, ". . . I am pained at my very heart: my heart maketh a noise in me." This deep groundswell of *desire*, this tidal motion of the life-floods is caused by the Holy Spirit. His work is never superficial, but always deep and inward.

> C. H. Spurgeon, *Metropolitan Tabernacle Pulpit*, Vol. 26, p. 223 [Romans 8:26–27; Psalm 38:9; Jeremiah 4:19]

Grace is as a fire in the soul, and he that has much of it . . . cannot but have a heart boiling with *earnestness*.

> C. H. Spurgeon

If we *long* to keep His statutes He will keep us; yea, His grace will keep us keeping His law.

> *Charles Spurgeon: The Best From All His Works*, p. 251

I had sooner that you believed half-a-dozen truths *intensely* than a hundred only feebly.

C. H. Spurgeon, *The Soul Winner*, p. 57

Your sermons—make them *red hot;* never mind if men say you are too *enthusiastic* or even too *fanatical.*

C. H. Spurgeon, *The Soul Winner*, p. 75

Oh, let us *long* to be used, pray to be used, and *pine* to be used!

C. H. Spurgeon, *The Soul Winner*, p. 312

True love is *intense*, its coals burn with *vehement heat*, it makes all things around it living.

C. H. Spurgeon, *Seven Wonders of Grace*, p. 71

I make bold to say that some men have been styled eccentric because they are really in *earnest*, and *earnestness* defies rules. I do not believe that it is possible for a man in downright *earnest* to be always "proper."

C. H. Spurgeon, *Eccentric Preachers*, p. 84

Were preachers more in *earnest* we should see more of what are called eccentricities, which are often only the ensigns of real zeal, and the tokens that a man is both natural and *intense.*

C. H. Spurgeon, *Eccentric Preachers*, p. 177

A *burning heart* will soon find for itself a flaming tongue.

C. H. Spurgeon, *Lectures to My Students*, p. 308

Supplication, in which a man's proper self is not thoroughly present in agonizing *earnestness* and vehement *desire*, is utterly ineffectual.

C. H. Spurgeon, *Morning and Evening*, p. 31 [Psalm 109:4; James 5:16]

Dr. Chalmers, after *kindling* churches and arousing nations to their duties, summed up his own attainments in the word "*desirousness,*" and took as the text that best described his inner state, that *passionate,* almost painful cry of David, "My soul breaketh for the *longing* that it hath unto Thy judgements."

> C. H. Spurgeon (quoting Alexander Raleigh), *The Treasury of David*, Vol. 3, pp. 183–184 [Psalm 119:20]

Earnestness is the life of supplication.

> C. H. Spurgeon

Prayers which are the offspring of *great desires* . . . are surely the work of the Holy Spirit.

> C. H. Spurgeon

Earnestness . . . is diminished by neglect of study.

> C. H. Spurgeon, *Lectures to My Students*, p. 310

Our *earnestness* must be kindled at an immortal flame.

> C. H. Spurgeon, *Lectures to My Students*, p. 313

Critics may take out their penknives to gore and gash, but honest hearts delight in the natural expressions, the instructive comparisons, and the heartfelt utterances of the *earnest* man whom the world sets down as an eccentric preacher.

> C. H. Spurgeon, *Eccentric Preachers*, p. 39

You are not only instructed, but influenced to *holy emotion,* and helped to express the same.

> C. H. Spurgeon, *Treasury of David*

True religion . . . has its *exclamations* and *raptures.*

> C. H. Spurgeon, *Treasury of David*

Amen has four meanings in Scripture. . . . "Lord, let it be so"—it is the heart's *desire.* . . . It means the affirmation of our faith. . . . It often expresses the joy of the heart. . . . It means, "I, in the name of God, solemnly pledge myself that in His strength I will seek to make it so; to Him be glory both now and for ever."

> C. H. Spurgeon, *The Treasury of the Bible*, Vol. 8, pp. 472–473
> [2 Peter 3:18]

Silent prayers are often true prayers, but there are times, in extremity of suffering, it is very helpful to give expression to the soul's agony. I know some friends who can never pray to their own comfort except they can hear their own voices; and I believe that it is a good thing for the most of us to retire to some private place where we cannot be heard by men, and where we can therefore freely use our voices in prayer. Very often, the use of the voice helps to keep the thoughts from wandering, and also gives *intensity* to the *desires*. You notice that David particularly mentions here that he cried unto the Lord with his voice. No doubt many of his prayers ascended to God from his heart without the medium of his voice; but here, the cry with voice went with the *desires* of his heart.

> C. H. Spurgeon, *Spurgeon's Expository Encyclopedia*, Vol. 15, p. 279 [Psalm 142:1]

The heart of preaching, the throwing of the soul into it, the *earnestness* which pleads as for life itself, is half the battle as to gaining attention. . . . Have something to say, and say it *earnestly*, and the congregation will be at your feet.

> C. H. Spurgeon, *Lectures to My Students*, p. 136

Doubt

Many a believer lives in the cottage of *doubt* when he might live in the mansion of faith.

> C. H. Spurgeon, *The Treasury of the Bible*, Vol. 3, p. 330 [Song of Solomon 2:10–13]

Have we clung to the naked promise of God and rested upon the bare arm of omnipotence, which in and of itself is more than sufficient for the fulfilment of every promise? O Lord, where are we? Where shall we find an oasis of faith amid this wilderness of *doubt?* Where shall we find an Abraham?

> C. H. Spurgeon, *The Treasury of the Bible*, Vol. 6, p. 71 [Luke 18:8]

"Down-Grade" Controversy

One of the perils of the hour is the failure of many good men to discern the peril.

> C. H. Spurgeon (quoting E. K. Alden, because his views were so similar to his own), *The Sword and the Trowel*, September 1888, *The "Down-Grade" Controversy*, p. 62

During the past year we have often had to look down from the royal road of the truth upon those craggy paths which others have chosen, which we feel will lead to destruction. We have had enough of the *"Down-Grade."* . . . What havoc false doctrine is making no tongue can tell.

> C. H. Spurgeon, *The "Down-Grade" Controversy*, p. 2

No loyal soldier could endure to see his Lord's cause so grievously wronged by traitors. Something will come of the struggle over the *"Down-Grade."* The Lord has designs in connection therewith which His adversaries little dream of. Meanwhile, it behoves all who love the Lord Jesus and His gospel to keep close together, and make a common cause against deadly error.

> C. H. Spurgeon, *The "Down-Grade" Controversy*, p. 3

The *"Down-Grade" Controversy* was one of the most significant disputes in the life of C. H. Spurgeon, occurring near the close of his comparatively short life of almost 58 years. It began in 1887 and continued on until—and even after—his death in 1892. He indicated in an editorial "note" in the very last days of his life that the *controversy* probably contributed to his early demise. He said: "To be free from all ecclesiastical entanglements is to the Christian minister a blessing worth all it has cost, even though an almost fatal illness might be reckoned as part of the price."

The Publisher, *The Sword and the Trowel*, February 1892, p. 93

Spurgeon was "a voice crying in the wilderness" during this period. His voice lives on to speak in written form, to other generations. His sermons are perhaps his greatest living legacy, but his strict adherence to Truth in this *controversy* also has lessons for us.

The Publisher, *The Sword and the Trowel*, February 1892, p. 93

In 1889, three years before his death, and in the midst of the *"Down-Grade" Controversy,* C. H. Spurgeon warned that *"debasing doctrine* now, will affect children yet unborn, generation after generation. . . . For my part, I am quite willing to be eaten by dogs for the next fifty years; but the more distant future shall vindicate me." A. W. Pink, then a child of three, was one of the few who was to remain a burning witness to historic Christianity in the wilderness years which followed. Though his life encircled the earth, and included preaching and writing in four countries—England, the United States, Australia, and Scotland—he was virtually unknown in the Christian world at the time of his death in 1952. Since then *the new era which Spurgeon anticipated* has dawned and Pink's magazine articles, now reissued by many publishers in book form, have been powerfully used of God.

Taken from the back cover of *The Life of Arthur W. Pink,* by Iain H. Murray

On the *"Down-Grade,"* the train travels fast. . . . A craven spirit is upon many, and their tongues are paralyzed. Oh, for an outburst of true faith and holy zeal!

C. H. Spurgeon, *The "Down-Grade" Controversy*, p. 76

The *"Down-Grade" Controversy* raised questions which are as important in the 1980s as they were in the 1880s. . . . C. H. Spurgeon has had many heirs over the last one hundred years. . . . Dr. D. M. Lloyd-Jones and those churches and church groupings associated with them . . . all affirmed that "fellowship with known and vital error is participation in sin."

R. J. Sheehan, *C. H. Spurgeon and the Modern Church*, p. 96

Eccentric

Critics may take out their penknives to gore and gash, but honest hearts delight in the natural expressions, the instructive comparisons, and the heartfelt utterances of the earnest man whom the world sets down as an *eccentric* preacher.

C. H. Spurgeon, *Eccentric Preachers*, p. 39

Now, in these cases the *eccentricity* lay in plain speaking, and this is an order of *eccentricity* of which we cannot very well have too much, if it be accompanied by sincere affection and tempered with gentleness.

C. H. Spurgeon, *Eccentric Preachers*, p. 79

I make bold to say that some men have been styled *eccentric* because they are really in earnest, and earnestness defies rules. I do not believe that it is possible for a man in downright earnest to be always "proper."

C. H. Spurgeon, *Eccentric Preachers*, p. 84

Were preachers more in earnest we should see more of what are called *eccentricities*, which are often only the ensigns of real zeal, and the tokens that a man is both natural and intense.

C. H. Spurgeon, *Eccentric Preachers*, p. 177

Some congregations are dying of dignity, and must be aroused by real life. . . . Bring the trumpet! Sound a blast and wake the sleepers! *Eccentric!* Yes, *eccentricity*, if you like to call life by that name. Heaven knows it is sadly wanted.

C. H. Spurgeon, *Eccentric Preachers*, p. 82

Election

True faith confesses Christ, and, at the same time, confesses its sin. There must be repentance of sin and acknowledgment of it before God if faith is to give proof of its truth. A faith that never had a tear in its eye, or a blush on its cheek, is not the faith of God's *elect*.

C. H. Spurgeon, *Seven Wonders of Grace*, p. 94

"Precious faith" . . . is the symbol of our *election*, the evidence of our calling, the root of all graces.

C. H. Spurgeon, *The Treasury of the Bible*, Vol. 8, p. 440
[2 Peter 1:1–4]

The Lord . . . *chose* me . . . surely this ought to make us in our very worst and dullest moments sing for joy.

C. H. Spurgeon, *Spurgeon's Expository Encyclopedia*, Vol. 10,
p. 46 [1 John 1:4; Ephesians 1:4; 1 Peter 1:8]

Error

We want churches that know the truth, and are well taught in the things of God. If we taught better they would learn better. See how little many professors know; not enough to give them discernment between living truth and

45

deadly error. Old-fashioned believers could give you chapter and verse for what they believed; but how few of such remain! To try to shake them was by no means a hopeful task: you might as well have hoped to shake the pillars of the universe; for they were steadfast, and could not be carried about with every wind of doctrine. They knew what they knew, and they held fast that which they had learned. Oh, for a church of out-and-out believers, impervious to the soul-destroying doubt which pours upon us in showers!

The Greatest Fight in the World, C. H. Spurgeon's "Final Manifesto," pp. 45–46 [Ephesians 4:14; Romans 6:17]

My topics have to do with our life-work, with the crusade against *error* and sin in which we are engaged. I hope that every man here is pledged to do and dare for Christ and for His cross, and never to be satisfied till Christ's foes are routed and Christ Himself is satisfied. Our fathers used to speak of "The Cause of God and Truth"; and it is for this that we bear arms, the few against the many, the feeble against the mighty. Oh, to be found good soldiers of Jesus Christ!

The Greatest Fight in the World, C. H. Spurgeon's "Final Manifesto," pp. 8–9

The "Down-Grade" Controversy raised questions which are as important in the 1980s as they were in the 1880s. . . . C. H. Spurgeon has had many heirs over the last one hundred years. . . . Dr. D. M. Lloyd-Jones and those churches and church groupings associated with them . . . all affirmed that "fellowship with known and vital *error* is participation in sin."

R. J. Sheehan, *C. H. Spurgeon and the Modern Church,* p. 96

Eternity

We are always writing on the pages of *eternity.*

Charles Spurgeon: The Best From All His Works, p. 132

Exhortation

Let us be thankful that some saints love us well enough to give themselves the pain and trouble of *exhorting* us. . . . It is well to stir [one another] up to greater zeal by a loving *exhortation.*

> C. H. Spurgeon, *Metropolitan Tabernacle Pulpit,* Vol. 36, p. 108 [Hebrews 3:13; 10:24–25]

Faith

Faith that does not obey is dead *faith*—nominal *faith.* . . . Sinner, if thou wilt be saved, thou must give thyself up to Jesus Christ to be His servant, and to do all that He bids thee.

> *Spurgeon's Expository Encyclopedia,* Vol. 7, p. 169 [James 2:20; Romans 10:17]

Faith is the great gospel grace. . . . True *faith* always prays, and when a man professes *faith* in the Lord Jesus and yet does not cry to the Lord daily, we dare not believe in his *faith* or his conversion.

> *The Best of C. H. Spurgeon,* p. 113

Faith gathers the handfuls of sacred corn from which contemplation threshes out the ears and prepares soul-sustaining bread.

> *The Best of C. H. Spurgeon,* p. 38

Faith enables us so to rejoice in the Lord that our infirmities become platforms for the display of His grace.

> C. H. Spurgeon, *An All-Round Ministry,* p. 16

Faith must obey her Saviour's will as well as trust His grace.

> C. H. Spurgeon, *An All-Round Ministry,* p. 379

Faith always sees the bow of covenant promise whenever sense sees the cloud of affliction.

> C. H. Spurgeon, *Faith's Checkbook*, p. 6 [Genesis 9:14]

The root of *faith* produces the flower of heart-joy.

> C. H. Spurgeon, *Faith's Checkbook*, p. 65 [Psalm 33:21]

A sight of Jesus by *faith* is the pleasure of beholding Him in His glory and being transformed into His image.

> C. H. Spurgeon, *Faith's Checkbook*, p. 67 [2 Corinthians 3:18]

Faith sees the clouds emptying themselves and making the little hills rejoice on every side.

> C. H. Spurgeon, *Faith's Checkbook*, p. 71 [Ecclesiastes 11:3]

Faith, having God with her, is in a clear majority.

> C. H. Spurgeon, *Faith's Checkbook*, p. 115 [2 Kings 6:16]

Faith sees God with a transforming look. . . . The glory of God in the face of Jesus Christ yields us Heaven below, and it will be to us the Heaven of Heaven above.

> C. H. Spurgeon, *Faith's Checkbook*, p. 139 [2 Corinthians 4:6]

By *faith* the wilderness can become the suburbs of Heaven, and the woods the vestibule of glory.

> C. H. Spurgeon, *Faith's Checkbook*, p. 169 [Ezekiel 34:25]

Grace . . . is the fountain and source even of *faith* itself. *Faith* is the work of God's grace in us. . . . *Faith*, which is coming to Christ, is the result of divine drawing. Grace is the first and last moving cause of salvation, and *faith*, important as it is, is only an important part of the machinery which grace employs. . . .

Faith occupies the position of a channel or conduit-pipe. Grace is the fountain and the stream: *faith* is the aqueduct along which the flood of mercy flows down to refresh the thirsty sons of men.

> C. H. Spurgeon, *Metropolitan Tabernacle Pulpit*, Vol. 27, p. 401 [Ephesians 2:8]

True *faith* confesses Christ, and, at the same time, confesses its sin. There must be repentance of sin and acknowledgment of it before God if *faith* is to give proof of its truth. A *faith* that never had a tear in its eye, or a blush on its cheek, is not the *faith* of God's elect.

> C. H. Spurgeon, *Seven Wonders of Grace*, p. 94

We are sinking by our struggles when we might float by *faith*. Oh, for grace to be quiet!

> C. H. Spurgeon, *Faith's Checkbook*, p. 174 [Isaiah 30:15]

Faith is like a shield, because it hath good need to be strong.

> C. H. Spurgeon, *The Treasury of the Bible*, Vol. 7, p. 450 [Ephesians 6:16]

Faith is like a shield because it is of no use except it be well handled.

> C. H. Spurgeon, *The Treasury of the Bible*, Vol. 7, p. 451 [Ephesians 6:16]

You will handle *faith* well if you are able to quote the promises of God against the attacks of your enemy.

> C. H. Spurgeon, *The Treasury of the Bible*, Vol. 7, p. 451 [Ephesians 6:16]

He who can live by *faith* shall have a constant supply of the oil of joy poured upon him by the Holy Spirit, and his mourning shall flee away.

> C. H. Spurgeon, *Spurgeon's Expository Encyclopedia*, Vol. 10, p. 61 [Isaiah 61:3]

Faith . . . may be compared to flying—"They shall mount up with wings as eagles." "I bear you as upon eagles' wings."

C. H. Spurgeon, The Treasury of the Bible, Vol. 7, p. 355
[Ephesians 1:19–23; Isaiah 40:31; Exodus 19:4]

Grow in that root-grace, *faith.* Believe the promises more firmly than you have done. Let *faith* increase in fulness, constancy, simplicity. . . . An increase of love to Jesus, and a more perfect apprehension of His love to us, is one of the best tests of growth in grace.

C. H. Spurgeon, Morning and Evening, p. 8 [2 Peter 3:18]

The believer every day takes venturesome flights into the atmosphere of Heaven . . . with no other wings but those of *faith* and love. Here is a continued and splendid miracle of the divine power.

C. H. Spurgeon, The Treasury of the Bible, Vol. 7, p. 355
[Ephesians 1:19–23; Isaiah 40:31; Exodus 19:4]

"Precious *faith*" . . . is the symbol of our election, the evidence of our calling, the root of all graces.

C. H. Spurgeon, The Treasury of the Bible, Vol. 8, p. 440
[2 Peter 1:1–4]

"Precious *faith*" . . . is the channel of communion, the weapon of prevalence, the shield of safety.

C. H. Spurgeon, The Treasury of the Bible, Vol. 8, p. 440
[2 Peter 1:1–4]

"Precious *faith*" . . . is the substance of hope, the evidence of eternity, . . . the passport of glory. O for more . . . precious *faith.*

C. H. Spurgeon, The Treasury of the Bible, Vol. 8, p. 440
[2 Peter 1:1–4]

I have often thought if I could have heard the way of *faith* simply stated, my soul would have leaped into liberty long before.

> C. H. Spurgeon, *Spurgeon's Expository Encyclopedia*, Vol. 8,
> p. 186 [Romans 10:17]

Faith is the bee that carries the pollen.

> C. H. Spurgeon, *Spurgeon's Expository Encyclopedia*, Vol. 15,
> p. 91 [Mark 16:14]

Faith is the Nazarite lock of Samson.

> C. H. Spurgeon, *Spurgeon's Expository Encyclopedia*, Vol. 15,
> p. 91 [Mark 16:14]

Patience is a pearl which is only found in the deep seas of affliction; and only grace can find it there, bring it to the surface, and adorn the neck of *faith* therewith.

> C. H. Spurgeon, *Metropolitan Tabernacle Pulpit*, Vol. 32,
> p. 314

Faith . . . muzzles the mouth of death.

> C. H. Spurgeon, *Spurgeon's Expository Encyclopedia*, Vol. 15,
> p. 92 [Hebrews 11:5]

We are persuaded to try the trembling legs of our *faith* by the sight of a promise.

> C. H. Spurgeon, *According to Promise*, p. 58 [Hebrews 11:8–
> 19]

By *faith* we realize the promise, and the foreshadowing of the expected blessing fills our souls with the benefit long before it actually comes.

> C. H. Spurgeon, *According to Promise*, p. 52 [Hebrews 11:8–
> 19]

Faith without a promise would be a foot without ground to stand upon.

> C. H. Spurgeon, *According to Promise*, p. 51 [Hebrews 11:8–
> 19]

Faith obliterates time, annihilates distance, and brings future things at once into its possession.

> C. H. Spurgeon, *According to Promise*, p. 52 [Hebrews 11:8–19]

The great father of the *faithful* saw the day of Christ through the telescope of God's promise, by the eye of *faith*.

> C. H. Spurgeon, *According to Promise*, p. 52 [Hebrews 11:8–19]

Where it is real, and can grasp a divine promise with firm grip, *faith* is a great wonder-worker.

> C. H. Spurgeon, *According to Promise*, p. 103 [Psalm 84:11]

We have not yet passed through the gates of pearl, nor have we trodden the streets of transparent gold; but the promise of such felicity lights up the gloom of our affliction, and yields us immediate foretastes of glory. We triumph by *faith* before our hands actually grasp the palm. We reign with Christ by *faith* before our heads are encircled with our unfading coronets.

> C. H. Spurgeon, *According to Promise*, p. 53 [Hebrews 11:8–19]

Many and many a time we have seen the dawn of Heaven while we have beheld light breaking from the promise. When *faith* has been vigorous we have climbed where Moses stood and gazed upon the land which flowed with milk and honey.

> C. H. Spurgeon, *According to Promise*, p. 53 [Hebrews 11:24–29]

Prayer takes the promise to the Bank of *Faith*, and obtains the golden blessing.

> C. H. Spurgeon, *According to Promise*, p. 69 [2 Peter 1:4]

Have you left the rut of present sensual perception for the way of *faith* in the unseen and eternal?

> C. H. Spurgeon, *According to Promise*, p. 19 [2 Corinthians 4:18]

God's smile beheld by *faith* gives us fulness of joy.

> C. H. Spurgeon, *According to Promise*, pp. 30–31 [Hebrews 11:8–19]

In a thousand ways . . . *faith* sweetens, enlarges, and enriches life.

> C. H. Spurgeon, *According to Promise*, p. 104 [Romans 5:1–5]

My *faith* not only flies to Heaven, but walks with God below.

> C. H. Spurgeon, *According to Promise*, p. 104 [Romans 5:1–5]

Faith receives more stabs from waverers than from avowed sceptics.

> C. H. Spurgeon, *The Treasury of the Bible*, Vol. 3, p. 84 [Psalm 119:162]

Faith has to bring all the faculties of the child of God upon their knees, and to say to them, "Be quiet; listen while God speaks." . . . "Wait, I say, on the Lord." May that which is written with ink in the Bible be written with grace on our hearts. May the public promise become a private promise to each one of us by the living experience of our own soul.

> C. H. Spurgeon, *The Treasury of the Bible*, Vol. 3, p. 85 [Psalm 119:162]

Many a believer lives in the cottage of doubt when he might live in the mansion of *faith*.

> C. H. Spurgeon, *The Treasury of the Bible*, Vol. 3, p. 330 [Song of Solomon 2:10–13]

Faith is the candlestick which holds the candle by which the chamber of thy heart is enlightened.

> C. H. Spurgeon, *The Treasury of the Bible*, Vol. 6, p. 69 [Luke 18:8]

The greatest believer would not *believe* for another moment unless grace were constantly given him to keep the flame of *faith* burning.

> C. H. Spurgeon, *The Treasury of the Bible*, Vol. 6, p. 69 [Luke 18:8]

The life of Jesus was a life of *faith—faith* which cried, "My God, My God," even when He was forsaken. His was, on a grander scale than ours, the battle of *faith* in the great Father, waged against all the rebellious influences which were in array against Him.

> C. H. Spurgeon, *The Treasury of the Bible*, Vol. 6, p. 69 [Luke 18:8; Matthew 27:46]

Divine truths, as they are written in the Book, and brought home to the heart by the Holy Ghost, are sure standing ground for that *faith* which Jesus looks for.

> C. H. Spurgeon, *The Treasury of the Bible*, Vol. 6, p. 73 [Luke 18:8]

Have we clung to the naked promise of God and rested upon the bare arm of omnipotence, which in and of itself is more than sufficient for the fulfillment of every promise? O Lord, where are we? Where shall we find an oasis of *faith* amid this wilderness of doubt? Where shall we find an Abraham?

> C. H. Spurgeon, *The Treasury of the Bible*, Vol. 6, p. 71 [Luke 18:8]

Believe up to the hilt. Plunge into this sea of holy confidence in God, and you shall find waters to swim in. . . . No man was ever yet found guilty of *believing* in God too much.

. . . Let us aspire to walk with God in the heavenlies, and become the King's Remembrancers.

> C. H. Spurgeon, *The Treasury of the Bible*, Vol. 6, p. 73 [Luke 18:8]

Let us seek grace to become importunate pleaders of a sort that cannot be denied, since their *faith* overcomes heaven by prayer.

> C. H. Spurgeon, *The Treasury of the Bible*, Vol. 6, p. 73 [Luke 18:8]

Virtues without *faith* are whitewashed sins.

> C. H. Spurgeon, *The New Park Street Pulpit*, Vol. 1, p. 21 [Romans 14:23]

Believing supplications are forecasts of the future. He who prayeth in *faith* is like the seer of old, he sees that which is yet to be: his holy expectancy, like a telescope, brings distant objects near to him, and things not seen as yet are visible to him.

> C. H. Spurgeon, *Metropolitan Tabernacle Pulpit*, Vol. 26, p. 227 [Romans 8:26–27]

The tail feathers of pride should be pulled out of our prayers, for they need only the wing feathers of *faith.*

> C. H. Spurgeon, *Metropolitan Tabernacle Pulpit*, Vol. 26, p. 224 [Romans 8:26–27]

I pray you, draw near to God, so that *faith* may become to you the mainspring of your life.

> C. H. Spurgeon, *Metropolitan Tabernacle Pulpit*, Vol. 27, p. 643 [Psalm 73:28]

Faith must abide, though joy depart.

> C. H. Spurgeon, *Metropolitan Tabernacle Pulpit*, Vol. 28, p. 620 [1 Corinthians 13:13]

Faith about my pain, my poverty, my despondency, my old age—that is *faith.*

> C. H. Spurgeon, *Metropolitan Tabernacle Pulpit*, Vol. 27,
> p. 643 [Psalm 73:28]

Faith is the work of God's grace in us.

> C. H. Spurgeon, *Metropolitan Tabernacle Pulpit*, Vol. 27,
> p. 401 [Ephesians 2:8]

Faith occupies the position of a channel or conduit-pipe. Grace is the fountain and the stream.

> C. H. Spurgeon, *Metropolitan Tabernacle Pulpit*, Vol. 27,
> p. 401 [Ephesians 2:8]

Faith is the aqueduct along which the flood of mercy flows down to refresh the thirsty sons of men.

> C. H. Spurgeon, *Metropolitan Tabernacle Pulpit*, Vol. 27,
> p. 401 [Ephesians 2:8]

Faith is precious, feeling is fickle. *Believing,* we stand firm; but by feeling we are tossed about.

> C. H. Spurgeon, *Metropolitan Tabernacle Pulpit*, Vol. 28, p. 62
> [Ephesians 2:10]

True feeling follows *faith,* and as such is valuable; but *faith* is the root, and the life of the tree lies there, and not in the boughs and leaves, which may be taken away, and yet the tree will survive.

> C. H. Spurgeon, *Metropolitan Tabernacle Pulpit*, Vol. 28,
> p. 620 [Ephesians 2:10]

What is *faith?* It is made up of three things—knowledge, belief, trust.

> C. H. Spurgeon, *All of Grace*, p. 44 [Romans 10:17]

Faith is an act of the understanding; but it also proceeds from the heart. God gives salvation to *faith* because it resides next door to the affections, and is near akin to love; and love is the parent and the nurse of every holy feeling and act. Love to God is obedience, love to God is holiness. To love God and to love man is to be conformed to the image of Christ; and this is salvation.

> C. H. Spurgeon, *All of Grace*, p. 62 [Romans 10:9; John 14:21]

To see the effects of the truth of God in the lives of holy men is confirmatory to *faith* and stimulating to holy aspiration.

> *The Greatest Fight in the World*, C. H. Spurgeon's "Final Manifesto," p. 20

Faith by cheering the heart keeps it free from the fear which, in times of pestilence, kills more than the plague itself.

> C. H. Spurgeon, *The Treasury of David*, Vol. 2, Pt. 2, p. 90 [Psalm 91:3]

False (Damning) Doctrine

We are very careful to use our best language when proclaiming eternal truths in this battle against *false doctrine*.

> *The Greatest Fight in the World*, C. H. Spurgeon's "Final Manifesto," p. 6 [1 John 2:4; Jude 3]

The Holy Spirit makes no promise to bless *compromises*. If we make a treaty with *error* or sin, we do it at our own risk. If we do anything that we are not clear about, if we tamper with truth or holiness, if we are friends of the world, if we make provision for the flesh, if we preach half-heartedly and are in league with *errorists*, we have no promise that the Holy Spirit will go with us. If you want to know what great things the Lord can do, as the Lord God Almighty, be separate from the world, and from those who apostatize from the truth. The man of God will have nothing to do with Sodom, or with *false doctrine*. If you see anything that is evil, give it the cut direct. Have done with those who have done with the truth.

The Greatest Fight in the World, C. H. Spurgeon's "Final
Manifesto," pp. 59–60 [Jude 3; James 3:17]

Oh, how the King is dishonoured by the mutilation and misrepresentation of His Word! Therefore, dear brethren, we are always bound to bear our protest against *false doctrine.* I am sometimes accused of saying sharp things. The charge does not come home to my conscience with very great power. If anybody said I spoke smooth things I think it would oppress me a great deal more. . . . It is time that somebody should believe something; and a little sharpness of speech might not only be excused, but commended, if we had but men who spoke what they did know, and testified honestly to the truth which they had received. Everyone here present, who is maintained from the King's palace, is bound to fight against *every doctrine which insults the King.*

Spurgeon's Expository Encyclopedia, Vol. 15, pp. 433–434
[Galatians 1:8–9; Ezra 4:14]

Great God . . . we long that *false doctrine* may fly like birds of darkness before the light of Thy coming.

C. H. Spurgeon, *C. H. Spurgeon's Prayers,* p. 68

Keep Thy sheep from the poisonous pastures of *error.*

Charles Spurgeon: The Best From All His Works, p. 226

The new views are not the old truth in better dress, but *deadly errors* with which we can have no fellowship. . . . I cannot endure *false doctrine,* however neatly it may be put before me. Would you have me eat poisoned meat because the dish is of the choicest ware?

C. H. Spurgeon [Jude 3; Galatians 1:8–9]

If I am wrong upon other points, I am positive that the sin of this age is *impurity of doctrine,* and laxity of faith. . . . A new age this, when *falsehood* and truth can kiss each other! New times these when fire and water can become friendly! Glorious times these when . . . heaven, *falsehood and error* are linked hand in hand.

> C. H. Spurgeon, *The New Park Street Pulpit*, Vol. 2, pp. 115–116 [Revelation 3:4; Jude 3; Galatians 1:8–9]

I am often asked, "Why do you not preach what you believe, and leave other people's doctrine alone?" Ah . . . Why don't I? And why did not the Lord Jesus Christ let the devil alone, and let false teachers alone; and why does not the gospel let *error* and *falsehood* alone? When the Lord Jesus Christ came into the world, one part of His work was to destroy the works of the devil.

> C. H. Spurgeon, *Spurgeon's Expository Encyclopedia*, Vol. 15, p. 164 [1 John 3:8]

Christ's faithful servants are to follow His example, to quarrel with *error*, to fight against sin, to be aggressive against everything that is opposed to our Lord and His truth.

> C. H. Spurgeon, *Spurgeon's Expository Encyclopedia*, Vol. 15, p. 164 [1 John 3:8; Exodus 32:26; Matthew 10:34]

We must not let *falsehood* and sin and *error* alone. Christ Himself said, "Think not that I am come to send peace on earth: I came not to send peace, but a sword" (Matthew 10:34).

> C. H. Spurgeon, *Spurgeon's Expository Encyclopedia*, Vol. 15, p. 164 [1 John 3:8; Exodus 32:36; Matthew 10:34]

During the past year we have often had to look down from the royal road of the truth upon those craggy paths which others have chosen, which we feel will lead to destruction. We have had enough of the "Down-Grade." . . . What havoc *false doctrine* is making no tongue can tell.

> C. H. Spurgeon, *The "Down-Grade" Controversy*, p. 2

Falsehood

What marvel if, under some men's shifty talk, people grow into love of both truth and *falsehood!* The fact is, they would like anything if only a clever deceiver would put it plausibly before them. They admire Moses and Aaron, but they would not say a word against Jannes and Jambres. We shall not join in the confederacy which seems to aim at such a comprehension. We must preach the gospel so distinctly that our people know what we are preaching. "If the trumpet give an uncertain sound, who shall prepare himself for the battle?" We shall not hesitate to speak in the strongest Saxon words we can find, and in the plainest sentences we can put together, that which we hold as fundamental truth.

The Greatest Fight in the World, C. H. Spurgeon's "Final Manifesto," pp. 38–39 [Jude 3; Galatians 1:8–9]

We want churches that know the truth, and are well taught in the things of God. If we taught better they would learn better. See how little many professors know; not enough to give them discernment between living truth and *deadly error.* Old-fashioned believers could give you chapter and verse for what they believed; but how few of such remain! To try to shake them was by no means a hopeful task: you might as well have hoped to shake the pillars of the universe; for they were steadfast, and could not be carried about with every wind of doctrine. They knew what they knew, and they held fast that which they had learned. Oh, for a church of out-and-out believers, impervious to the soul-destroying doubt which pours upon us in showers!

The Greatest Fight in the World, C. H. Spurgeon's "Final Manifesto," pp. 45–46 [Ephesians 4:14; Romans 6:17]

The Holy Spirit will never set His seal to *falsehood.* Never! If what you preach is not the truth, God will not own it. If we do not speak clear doctrine with plainness of speech, the Holy Spirit will not put His signature to our empty prating.

> *The Greatest Fight in the World,* C. H. Spurgeon's "Final Manifesto," p. 61

Fear

No sooner is the soul *quickened* than it at once discovers its *lost estate,* is *horrified thereat,* looks out for a refuge, and believing Christ to be a suitable one, flies to Him and reposes in Him.

> C. H. Spurgeon, *Words of Warning for Daily Life,* pp. 69–70

The period of my conviction of sin is burned into my memory as with a red-hot iron. Its wounds are cured, but the scars remain. There I stood, *fearing* every moment lest I should be crushed into the abyss and justly lost forever.

> C. H. Spurgeon, *Metropolitan Tabernacle Pulpit,* Vol. 18, p. 485

Faith by cheering the heart keeps it free from the *fear* which, in times of pestilence, kills more than the plague itself.

> C. H. Spurgeon, *The Treasury of David,* Vol. 2, Pt. 2, p. 90 [Psalm 91:3]

Feeling

Faith is precious, *feeling* is fickle. Believing, we stand firm; but by *feeling* we are tossed about.

> C. H. Spurgeon, *Metropolitan Tabernacle Pulpit,* Vol. 28, p. 62 [Ephesians 2:10]

True *feeling* follows faith, and as such is valuable; but faith is the root, and the life of the tree lies there, and not in the boughs and leaves, which may be taken away, and yet the tree will survive.

> C. H. Spurgeon, *Metropolitan Tabernacle Pulpit*, Vol. 28,
> p. 620 [Ephesians 2:10]

Fellowship (Communion)

Holy *fellowship* brings heavenly joy.

> C. H. Spurgeon, *Spurgeon's Expository Encyclopedia*, Vol. 10,
> p. 63 [Isaiah 61:3]

A drop of glory is sweet, but, oh, to taste a joy that is full of glory—is that possible here? Ay, and some of us bear witness that it is so: we have felt joy that we dare not tell, and could not tell if we dared: men would turn again and rend us, condemning us as utterly fanatical or out of our minds if we were to cast these pearls before them; but, oh, if they could guess what delicious draughts are held within the jewelled chalice of divine *communion* they would be ready to wade through hell itself to drink from it. Our joy is altogether unspeakable joy at times.

> C. H. Spurgeon, *Metropolitan Tabernacle Pulpit*, Vol. 27, p. 78
> [Galatians 5:22; 1 Peter 1:8; Jeremiah 15:16]

The oil of joy is poured out in . . . *fellowship.*

> C. H. Spurgeon, *Spurgeon's Expository Encyclopedia*, Vol. 10,
> p. 62 [Isaiah 61:3; 1 John 1:1–4]

Precious Lord Jesus, let me in very deed know the blessedness which dwells in abiding, unbroken *fellowship* with Thee. I am a poor worthless one, whose cheek Thou hast deigned to kiss! O let me kiss Thee in return with the kisses of my lips.

> C. H. Spurgeon, *Morning and Evening*, p. 244 [Song of
> Solomon 1:2; 5:13]

Fruit

The vine is constantly used in Scripture as a picture of the nominal Church of Christ; so, like the vine, we must either bring forth *fruit* or we shall be accounted good for nothing. . . . We must bear *fruit*, or we shall certainly perish.

C. H. Spurgeon, *We Endeavour,* pp. 89–90

A tree of the Lord's right-hand planting bears *fruit* to His honour and glory, visible to those who are round about him.

C. H. Spurgeon, *Flowers From a Puritan's Garden,* p. 100
[James 2:22 NEB]

Lord . . . Make my inward grace to be so vigorous that my outer life may be *fruitful to Thy praise.*

C. H. Spurgeon, *Flowers From a Puritan's Garden,* p. 100

Giving

Our *gifts* are not to be measured by the amount we *contribute,* but by the surplus kept in our own hand.

C. H. Spurgeon, *Metropolitan Tabernacle Pulpit,* Vol. 37,
p. 625 [2 Corinthians 8; Luke 21:1–4]

Glory

"The Lord will give grace." You may have it; therefore desire it, long for it, seek it, prize it; and you shall . . . have it. . . . *Glory* is really nothing more than grace fully developed. . . . The Lord gives his people the grace to live a heavenly life before they get to heaven; he gives them the grace to taste the clusters of Eschol before they enter the Promised Land; and he will continue to give grace till grace is consummated in *glory.*

Spurgeon's Expository Encyclopedia, Vol. 8, p. 235 [Psalm 84:11]

Grace is *glory* in the bud.

C. H. Spurgeon

Let us gaze upon Thy *glory* till we are transformed by the sight and become Christlike among the sons of men.

C. H. Spurgeon, *Best of C. H. Spurgeon,* p. 97

In a word, by faith we behold the *glory* of the Lord as in a glass, and we are changed into the same image—and the image of God is love.

C. H. Spurgeon, *Complete in Christ and Love's Logic,* p. 106

Glory is eternal love making itself known to man through saving and sustaining grace.

Author unknown, probably Charles Spurgeon

The *glory* of the divine Trinity overawes us until we behold the milder radiance of the Incarnate God.

C. H. Spurgeon, *According to Promise,* p. 125 [2 Corinthians 1:20]

There is more of God's *glory and majesty* to be seen in the manger and the cross, than in the sparkling stars above, the rolling deep below, the towering mountain, the teeming valleys, the abodes of life, or the abyss of death. Let us then give ourselves up to holy wonder, such as will produce gratitude, worship, love, and confidence, as we think of that great "mystery of godliness, God manifest in the flesh."

C. H. Spurgeon, *Christ's Incarnation,* front cover [1 Timothy 3:16; John 1:14]

We have not yet passed through the gates of pearl, nor have we trodden the streets of transparent gold; but the promise of such felicity lights up the gloom of our affliction, and yields us immediate foretastes of *glory.* We triumph by faith before our hands actually grasp the palm. We reign with Christ by faith before our heads are encircled with our unfading coronets.

> C. H. Spurgeon, *According to Promise*, p. 53 [Hebrews 11:8–19]

Praise is the rehearsal of our eternal song. By grace we learn to sing, and in *glory* we continue to sing.

> C. H. Spurgeon, *Metropolitan Tabernacle Pulpit*, Vol. 36, p. 12 [Psalm 103:1]

God's Economy of Words

There is always in the utterance of the Divine One a great depth which coucheth beneath. Our words, if they give one sense, do well, but the Lord knoweth how to speak so that He shall teach many truths in *few words*. We give little in much; God giveth much in little. . . . *Few words* and much meaning—this is the rule with God. . . . God droppeth pearls from His lips each time He speaketh to us; nor shall we, perhaps, even in eternity, know how divine are God's words—how like Himself, how exceeding broad, how infinite.

> C. H. Spurgeon, *Teachings of Nature in the Kingdom of Grace*, p. 14

God's Gifted Communion of Saints

Spurgeon found himself living with God's Word and *its interpreters*. Anything and everything that made God clear to the heart was relevant to Charles Spurgeon.

> *Devotions and Prayers of Charles H. Spurgeon*, first page of Preface

Use all means and helps towards the understanding of the Scriptures. When Philip asked the Ethiopian eunuch whether he understood the prophecy of Isaiah, he replied, "How can I, unless *some man* should guide me?" . . . Some

65

under the pretence of being taught of the Spirit of God, refuse to be instructed by *books* or by *living men.* This is no honouring of the Spirit of God; it is a disrespect to Him, for if He gives to some of His servants more light than to others—and it is clear He does—then they are bound to give that light to others, and to use it for the good of the church. But if the other part of the church refuse to receive that light, to what end did the Spirit of God give it? This would imply that there is a mistake somewhere in the economy of *gifts and graces,* which is managed by the Holy Spirit. . . . It would be most wicked of us to say, "We will not have the heavenly treasure which exists in earthen vessels."

C. H. Spurgeon, Words of Counsel for Christian Workers,
pp. 112–113

Both Paul and Tyndale requested *books* as their companions as they awaited trial and certain death. Charles Spurgeon had a marvelous comment on Paul's request:

"He is inspired, yet he wants *books!* He has been preaching at least for 30 years, yet he wants *books!* He has seen the Lord, and yet he wants *books!* He has had a wider experience than most men, yet he wants *books!* He had been caught up into the third heaven, and had heard things which it is unlawful for a man to utter, yet he wants *books!* He had written the major part of the New Testament, yet he wants *books!*"

How I wish that this same desire for *good books* characterized more believers today!

Victorious Christians You Should Know, p. 8 [2 Timothy 4:13]

Gospel

We can learn nothing of the *gospel* except by feeling its truths.

The Best of C. H. Spurgeon, p. 49 [John 14:21]

Though nowadays we hear of persons being healed before they have been wounded and brought into a certainty of justification without ever having lamented their condemnation, we are very dubious as to the value of such healings and justifyings. This style of things is not according to the truth. God never clothes men until He has first stripped them, nor does He quicken them by the *gospel* till first they are slain by the *law*. When you meet with persons in whom there is no trace of conviction of sin, you may be quite sure that they have not been wrought upon by the Holy Spirit, for "when He is come, He will reprove the world of sin, and of righteousness, and of judgment." Great care must be taken that faith is exercised upon Christ for a *complete salvation* and not for a part of it.

> *The Best of C. H. Spurgeon*, p. 111[2 Corinthians 5:20–21 *The Living Bible*]

Still the *gospel* breaks, and still it makes whole; still it wounds, and still it quickens; still it seems to hurl men down to hell in their terrible experience of the evil of sin, but still it lifts them up into an ecstatic joy, till they are exalted almost to Heaven when they lay hold upon it, and feel its power in their souls. The *gospel* that was a *gospel* of births and deaths, of killing and making alive, in the days of John Bunyan, has just the same effect upon our hearts today, when it comes with the power that God has put into it by His Spirit. It produces the same results, and the same sanctifying influence as it ever had.

> C. H. Spurgeon, *Metropolitan Tabernacle Pulpit*, Sermon No. 2,358, p. 198 [Hebrews 13:8; 2 Corinthians 5:20–21 *The Living Bible*]

I will not believe that you have tasted of the honey of the *gospel* if you keep it all to yourself. True grace puts an end to all spiritual monopoly.

> C. H. Spurgeon, *Day by Day with C. H. Spurgeon*, Compiled by
> Al Bryant, p. 158 [John 1:41]

Grace

All *grace* grows as love to the Word of God grows.

> C. H. Spurgeon (quoting Matthew Henry)

Holy activity is the mother of holy joy. Growth in *grace*, too, is a fount of true delight. Never is a believer happier than when he grows in *grace*.

> C. H. Spurgeon, *Spurgeon's Expository Encyclopedia*, Vol. 10,
> p. 49 [1 John 1:4]

Grace is always followed by immediate and continuous spiritual life.

> C. H. Spurgeon

Let God's *grace* just open a window and let the light into a man's soul, and he will stand astonished to see at what a distance he is from God.

> C. H. Spurgeon, *Pearls From Many Seas*, Compiled by
> Rev. J. B. McClure

Faith enables us so to rejoice in the Lord that our infirmities become platforms for the display of His *grace*.

> C. H. Spurgeon, *All-Round Ministry*, p. 16

Our troubles . . . are the dark chariots of bright *grace*.

> C. H. Spurgeon, *Devotions and Prayers of C. H. Spurgeon*,
> p. 26

Oh Lord . . . raise Thy faithful servants to a height of *grace* and holiness which shall be clearly supernatural.

> C. H. Spurgeon, *Faith's Checkbook*, p. 162

He who has most *grace* is most conscious of his need of more *grace*.

C. H. Spurgeon, *Metropolitan Tabernacle Pulpit*, Vol. 29, p. 454

Grace is as a fire in the soul, and he that hath much of it . . . cannot but have a heart boiling with earnestness.

C. H. Spurgeon

True fathers in *grace* meditate upon Christ; they feed upon Scripture, press the juice of it, and inwardly enjoy the flavor of it.

C. H. Spurgeon

Patience is a pearl which is only found in the deep seas of affliction; and only *grace* can find it there, bring it to the surface, and adorn the neck of faith therewith.

C. H. Spurgeon, *Metropolitan Tabernacle Pulpit*, Vol. 32, p. 314

"The Lord will give *grace*." You may have it; therefore desire it, long for it, seek it, prize it; and you shall . . . have it. . . . Glory is really nothing more than *grace* fully developed. . . . The Lord gives His people the *grace* to live a heavenly life before they get to heaven; He gives them the *grace* to taste the clusters of Eschol before they enter the Promised Land; and He will continue to give *grace* till *grace* is consummated in glory.

Spurgeon's Expository Encyclopedia, Vol. 8, p. 235 [Psalm 84:11]

Grace is glory in the bud.

C. H. Spurgeon

The most experienced saints bewail the weakness of every form of speech to describe the exceeding riches of the *grace* of God.

> C. H. Spurgeon, *Metropolitan Tabernacle Pulpit*, Vol. 28,
> p. 343 [Ephesians 2:7]

This is the holy reasoning of love; it draws no license from *grace*, but rather feels the strong constraints of gratitude leading it to holiness.

> C. H. Spurgeon, *The Treasury of the Bible*, Vol. 7, p. 736
> [Psalm 107:1, 8, 15, 21, 31]

Gather golden sheaves of *grace*, for they await you in the fields of faith.

> C. H. Spurgeon, *Day by Day with C. H. Spurgeon*, Compiled by
> Al Bryant, p. 136 [Matthew 19:26; Mark 9:23]

I will not believe that you have tasted of the honey of the gospel if you keep it all to yourself. True *grace* puts an end to all spiritual monopoly.

> C. H. Spurgeon, *Day by Day with C. H. Spurgeon*, Compiled by
> Al Bryant, p. 158 [John 1:41]

Bottomless mines are the treasures of divine *grace:*— Deep as our helpless miseries are, and boundless as our sins.

> C. H. Spurgeon, *Able to the Uttermost*, p. 120 [Ephesians 1:6]

If we long to keep His statutes He will keep us; yea, His *grace* will keep us keeping His law.

> *Charles Spurgeon: The Best From All His Works*, p. 251

Grow in that root-*grace*, faith. Believe the promises more firmly than you have done. Let faith increase in fulness, constancy, simplicity. . . . An increase in love to Jesus, and a more perfect apprehension of His love to us, is one of the best tests of growth in *grace*.

> C. H. Spurgeon, *Morning and Evening*, p. 8 [2 Peter 3:18]

Lord . . . Make my inward *grace* to be so vigorous that my outer life may be fruitful to Thy praise.

> C. H. Spurgeon, *Flowers From a Puritan's Garden*, p. 100

Praise is the rehearsal of our eternal song. By *grace* we learn to sing, and in glory we continue to sing.

> C.H. Spurgeon, *Metropolitan Tabernacle Pulpit*, Vol. 36, p. 12
> [Psalm 103:1]

Gratitude

The heart must be alive with gracious *gratitude,* or the leaf cannot long be green with living holiness.

> C. H. Spurgeon, *Flowers From a Puritan's Garden*, p. 104

This is the holy reasoning of love; it draws no license from grace, but rather feels the strong constraints of *gratitude* leading it to holiness.

> C. H. Spurgeon, *The Treasury of the Bible*, Vol. 7,
> p. 736 [Psalm 107:1, 8, 15, 21, 31]

Groaning

A *groan* is a matter about which there is no hypocrisy.

> C. H. Spurgeon, *Metropolitan Tabernacle Pulpit*, Vol. 26,
> p. 223 [Romans 8:26–27; Psalm 38:9]

Beloved, what a different view of prayer God has from that which men think to be the correct one. . . . To Him fine language is as sounding brass or a tinkling cymbal, but a *groan* has music in it.

> C. H. Spurgeon, *Metropolitan Tabernacle Pulpit*, Vol. 26,
> p. 223

"Maketh intercession for us." . . . By this expression it cannot be meant that the Holy Spirit ever *groans* or personally prays; but that He excites intense desire and creates unutterable *groanings* in us.

> C. H. Spurgeon, *Metropolitan Tabernacle Pulpit*, Vol. 26,
> p. 220 [Romans 8:26–27; Psalm 38:9]

I bow with reverent amazement, my heart sinking into the dust with adoration, when I reflect that God the Holy Ghost helps us when we cannot speak, but only *groan.* Yes, and when we cannot even utter our *groanings,* He doth not only help us but He claims as His own particular creation the "*groanings* that cannot be uttered." This is condescension indeed!

> C. H. Spurgeon, *Metropolitan Tabernacle Pulpit*, Vol. 26,
> p. 228 [Romans 8:26–27; Psalm 38:9]

A *groan* cometh not from the lips, but from the heart. A *groan* then is a part of prayer which we owe to the Holy Ghost, and the same is true of all the prayer which wells up from the deep fountains of our inner life. The prophet cried, ". . . I am pained at my very heart: my heart maketh a noise in me." This deep groundswell of desire, this tidal motion of the life-floods is caused by the Holy Spirit. His work is never superficial, but always deep and inward.

> C. H. Spurgeon, *Metropolitan Tabernacle Pulpit*, Vol. 26,
> p. 223 [Romans 8:26–27; Psalm 38:9; Jeremiah 4:19]

Heaven

One hour with Christ is worth an eternity of all earth's joys; and communion with Him is the best, the surest, and the most ecstatic foretaste of the bliss of *Heaven.*

> C. H. Spurgeon, *Gleanings Among the Sheaves*, p. 41

How can I have hope that *Heaven* shall be my eternal inheritance, unless the earnest be begun in my own soul on earth?

> C. H. Spurgeon, *Gleanings Among the Sheaves*, p. 95

My witness is, that those who are honoured of their Lord in public have usually to endure a secret chastening, or carry a peculiar cross, lest by any means they exalt themselves, and fall into the snare of the devil. Glory to God for the furnace, the hammer, and the file. *Heaven* shall be all the fuller of bliss because we have been filled with anguish here below, and earth shall be better tilled because of our training in the school of adversity.

C. H. Spurgeon, *Lectures to My Students*, p. 164

Faith sees God with a transforming look. . . . The glory of God in the face of Jesus Christ yields us *Heaven* below, and it will be to us the *Heaven of Heaven* above.

C. H. Spurgeon, *Faith's Checkbook*, p. 139 [2 Corinthians 4:6]

By faith the wilderness can become the suburbs of *Heaven*, and the woods the vestibule of glory.

C. H. Spurgeon, *Faith's Checkbook*, p. 169 [Ezekiel 34:25]

The believer every day takes venturesome flights into the atmosphere of *Heaven* . . . with no other wings but those of faith and love. Here is a continued and splendid miracle of the divine power.

C. H. Spurgeon, *The Treasury of the Bible*, Vol. 7, p. 355
[Ephesians 1:19–23; Isaiah 40:31; Exodus 19:4]

Many and many a time we have seen the dawn of *Heaven* while we have beheld light breaking from the promise. When faith has been vigorous we have climbed where Moses stood and gazed upon the land which flowed with milk and honey.

C. H. Spurgeon, *According to Promise*, p. 53 [Hebrews 11:24–29]

My faith not only flies to *Heaven*, but walks with God below.

C. H. Spurgeon, *According to Promise*, p. 104 [Romans 5:1–5]

The Holy Spirit is not only the pledge but the foretaste of everlasting bliss. . . . His influence over us brings us that same communion with God which we shall enjoy for ever in *Heaven*. . . . The possession of the Spirit is the dawn of glory.

C. H. Spurgeon, *My Sermon Notes*, Vol. 4, p. 269 [Ephesians 1:13–14]

Hell

Many unconverted men have a belief which is similar to faith, and yet it is not true faith. . . . It is to be feared that many are already mistaken, and will never discover their delusion till they lift up their eyes in the *world of woe*, where their disappointment will be terrible indeed.

C. H. Spurgeon, *According to Promise*, pp. 3–4

Lord, keep us right, true in doctrine, true in experience, true in life, true in word, true in deed. Let us have an intense agony of spirit concerning the many who are going down to the *everlasting fire* of which our Master spoke. Lord, save them! LORD, SAVE THEM!

C. H. Spurgeon, *C. H. Spurgeon's Prayers*, p. 17 [Luke 19:10]

Are YOU sure that you have it? It will be an awful thing to cry, "Peace, peace," where there is no peace, and to prophesy smooth things for yourself, and make your heart easy, and lull your conscience to slumber, and never to wake out of sleep till a clap of the thunder of judgment shall startle you out of presumption into *endless horror*.

C. H. Spurgeon, *According to Promise*, p. 4

Heresy

Fellowship with known and *vital error* is participation in sin.

John Blanchard (quoting C. H. Spurgeon), *More Gathered Gold*, p. 146

We should guard ourselves against *compromising the truth* of God by association with those who do not hold it, especially at such a time as this.

> C. H. Spurgeon, *Spurgeon's Sermons Preached on Unusual Occasions*, p. 216 [Romans 16:17; James 3:17]

Higher Truths

There are choice and precious doctrines of God's Word which are locked up in such cases as Leviticus or Solomon's Song, and you cannot get at them without a deal of unlocking of doors; and the Holy Spirit Himself must be with you, or else you will never come at the priceless treasure. The *higher truths* are as choicely hidden away as the precious regalia of princes; therefore, *search* as well as read.

> C. H. Spurgeon, *Spurgeon's Expository Encyclopedia*, Vol. 15, pp. 214–215 [Matthew 12:3–7]

Holiness

He has no *holiness* who thinks that he is *holy* enough. . . . The *holiest* minister is the man who cries, "O wretched man that I am! who shall deliver me from the body of this death?" No common Christian sighs in that fashion. Sin becomes exquisitely painful only to the exquisitely pure.

> C. H. Spurgeon, *An All-Round Ministry*, p. 252 [Matthew 5:8]

Holiness . . . should walk hand-in-hand with doctrinal orthodoxy.

> C. H. Spurgeon, *An All-Round Ministry*, p. 310

Come, Holy Spirit, we do know Thee; Thou hast often overshadowed us. Come, more fully take possession of us. Standing now as we feel we are right up at the mercy seat, our very highest prayer is for perfect *holiness*, complete consecration, entire cleansing from every evil. Take our heart, our head, our hands, our feet, and use us all for Thee. Lord, take our substance. . . . Take our talent. . . . Let every gain of mental attainment be still that we may serve Thee better.

> C. H. Spurgeon, *C. H. Spurgeon's Prayers*, pp. 3–4 [Hebrews 12:14, 29: 1 Peter 1:16]

The heart must be alive with gracious gratitude, or the leaf cannot long be green with living *holiness*.

> C. H. Spurgeon, *Flowers From a Puritan's Garden*, p. 104

This is the *holy* reasoning of love; it draws no license from grace, but rather feels the strong constraints of gratitude leading it to *holiness*.

> C. H. Spurgeon, *The Treasury of the Bible*, Vol. 7, p. 736 [Hebrews 12:14, 29; 1 Peter 1:16]

Oh Lord . . . raise Thy faithful servants to a height of *grace* and *holiness* which shall be clearly supernatural.

> C. H. Spurgeon, *Faith's Checkbook*, p. 162

Holy Spirit

The *Holy Spirit* will never set His seal to falsehood. Never! If what you preach is not the truth, God will not own it. If we do not speak clear doctrine with plainness of speech, the *Holy Spirit* will not put His signature to our empty prating.

> *The Greatest Fight in the World*, C. H. Spurgeon's "Final Manifesto," p. 61

I bow with reverent amazement, my heart sinking into the dust with adoration, when I reflect that God the *Holy Ghost* helps us when we cannot speak, but only groan. Yes, and when we cannot even utter our groanings, He doth not only help us but He claims as His own particular creation the "groanings that cannot be uttered." This is condescension indeed!

> C. H. Spurgeon, *Metropolitan Tabernacle Pulpit*, Vol. 26, p. 228 [Romans 8:26–27; Psalm 38:9]

There are certain people who think if they read a good long bit of Bible, they've done a great deal. . . . The mere outward fashion and form of Bible reading will not profit anybody. One bit of Bible prayed over, and bedewed with the *Spirit*, and made alive, though it be only a short sentence of six words, will profit you more than a hundred chapters without the *Spirit*, because the hundred chapters without the *Spirit* are flesh—dead; but the one verse with the *Spirit* is the thing that quickeneth.

[Compiler's shortened paraphrase—Better six words of one verse bedewed with the *Holy Spirit* than to routinely read one hundred chapters of the Bible.]

C. H. Spurgeon, *The Best of C. H. Spurgeon*, p. 218

The *Holy Spirit* makes no promise to bless compromises. If we make a treaty with error or sin, we do it at our own risk. If we do anything that we are not clear about, if we tamper with truth or holiness, if we are friends of the world, if we make provision for the flesh, if we preach half-heartedly and are in league with errorists, we have no promise that the *Holy Spirit* will go with us. If you want to know what great things the Lord can do, as the Lord God Almighty, be separate from the world, and from those who apostatize from the truth. The man of God will have nothing to do with Sodom, or with false doctrine. If you see anything that is evil, give it the cut direct. Have done with those who have done with the truth.

The Greatest Fight in the World, C. H. Spurgeon's "Final Manifesto," pp. 59–60

Divine truths, as they are written in the Book, and brought home to the heart by the *Holy Ghost*, are sure standing ground for that faith which Jesus looks for.

C. H. Spurgeon, *The Treasury of the Bible*, Vol. 6, p. 73 [Luke 18:8]

The *Holy Spirit* is the guarantee of everlasting joy.

> C. H. Spurgeon, *Metropolitan Tabernacle Pulpit*, Vol. 32,
> p. 323 [Romans 5:5; 15:13]

Though nowadays we hear of persons being healed before they have been wounded and brought into a certainty of justification without ever having lamented their condemnation, we are very dubious as to the value of such healings and justifyings. This style of things is not according to the truth. God never clothes men until He has first stripped them, nor does He quicken them by the gospel till first they are slain by the law. When you meet with persons in whom there is no trace of conviction of sin, you may be quite sure that they have not been wrought upon by the *Holy Spirit,* for "when He is come, He will reprove the world of sin, and of righteousness, and of judgment." Great care must be taken that faith is exercised upon Christ for a complete salvation and not for a part of it.

> *The Best of C. H. Spurgeon*, p. 111

Oh, to *burn* in our secret heart while we blaze before the eyes of others! This is the work of the *Spirit of God.* Work it in us, O adorable *Comforter!*

> C. H. Spurgeon, *Lectures to My Students*, p. 193

The *Holy Spirit* is not only the pledge but the foretaste of everlasting bliss. . . . His influence over us brings us that same communion with God which we shall enjoy for ever in Heaven. . . . This possession of the *Spirit* is the dawn of glory.

> C. H. Spurgeon, *My Sermon Notes*, Vol. 4, p. 269 [Ephesians
> 1:13–14]

Use all means and helps towards the understanding of the Scriptures. When Philip asked the Ethiopian eunuch whether he understood the prophecy of Isaiah, he replied,

"How can I, unless some man should guide me?" . . . Some under the pretence of being taught of the *Spirit of God,* refuse to be instructed by books or by living men. This is no honouring of the *Spirit of God;* it is a disrespect to Him, for if He gives to some of His servants more light than to others—and it is clear he does—then they are bound to give that light to others, and to use it for the good of the church. But if the other part of the church refuse to receive that light, to what end did the *Spirit of God* give it? This would imply that there is a mistake somewhere in the economy of the gifts and graces, which is managed by the *Holy Spirit.* . . . It would be most wicked of us to say, "We will not have the heavenly treasure which exists in earthen vessels."

C. H. Spurgeon, *Words of Counsel for Christian Workers,*
pp. 112–113

"Maketh intercession for us." . . . By this expression it cannot be meant that the *Holy Spirit* ever groans or personally prays; but that He excites intense desire and creates unutterable groanings in us.

C. H. Spurgeon, *Metropolitan Tabernacle Pulpit,* Vol. 26,
p. 220 [Romans 8:26–27; Psalm 38:9]

A groan cometh not from the lips, but from the heart. A groan then is a part of prayer which we owe to the *Holy Ghost,* and the same is true of all the prayer which wells up from the deep fountains of our inner life. The prophet cried, ". . . I am pained at my very heart: my heart maketh a noise in me." This deep groundswell of desire, this tidal motion of the life-floods is caused by the *Holy Spirit.* His work is never superficial, but always deep and inward.

C. H. Spurgeon, *Metropolitan Tabernacle Pulpit,* Vol. 26,
p. 223 [Romans 8:26–27; Psalm 38:9; Jeremiah 4:19]

Hope

Confident *hope* breeds inward joy.

C. H. Spurgeon, *Metropolitan Tabernacle Pulpit*, Vol. 32,
p. 323 [Romans 5:5; 15:13]

Let us make worldlings know the fragrance of our joyous
hope.

C. H. Spurgeon, *Metropolitan Tabernacle Pulpit*, Vol. 32,
p. 323 [Romans 5:5; 15:13; 2 Corinthians 2:14 (Moffatt)]

Hypocrisy

Secret religion is the very soul of godliness. What we are
alone, that alone we are. Private communion with Jesus is a
better sign of grace than all the outward sacraments that
were ever attended. It is not likely that a *hypocrite* will delight in solitary devotion; there is nothing in it to pay him for
his trouble; for his reward is the praise of man. Judgment
upon ourselves will be much more likely to be correct, if we
examine our hidden life than if we measure ourselves by
that which is seen of men.

C. H. Spurgeon, *Flowers From a Puritan's Garden*, p. 172

A groan is a matter about which there is no *hypocrisy.*

C. H. Spurgeon, *Metropolitan Tabernacle Pulpit*, Vol. 26,
p. 223 [Romans 8:26–27; Psalm 38:9]

Idleness, Laziness

"If ye do not go forth to the battles of the Lord, and contend for the Lord God and for His people, ye do sin against
the Lord: and be sure your sin will find you out." The sin of
doing nothing is about the biggest of all sins, for it involves
most of the others. . . . Horrible *idleness!* God save us from
it!

C. H. Spurgeon, *Words of Wisdom for Daily Life*, pp. 136–137
[Numbers 32:20–23; Jude 3; Ephesians 6:17]

A man cannot be *idle* and yet have Christ's sweet company. Christ is a quick walker, and when His people would talk with Him they must travel quickly too, or else they will soon lose His company.

> C. H. Spurgeon, *Words of Wisdom for Daily Life*, p. 55 [John 9:4]

The manna which the children of Israel kept till morning bred worms and stank: *idle grace* would soon become active corruption.

> C. H. Spurgeon, *Words of Wisdom for Daily Life*, p. 55 [John 9:4]

Sloth hardens the conscience: *laziness* is one of the irons with which the heart is seared.

> C. H. Spurgeon, *Words of Wisdom for Daily Life*, p. 55 [John 9:4]

O friends, it is a sad thing to rust the edge off from one's mind, and to lose keenness of moral perception; but *sloth* will surely do this for us. David felt the emasculating power of *sloth*, he was losing the force of his conscience, and was ready for anything . . . lust . . . murder.

> C. H. Spurgeon, *Words of Wisdom for Daily Life*, p. 56 [2 Samuel 11:1]

An *idler* has no right in the pulpit. He is an instrument of Satan in damning the souls of men. The ministry demands brain labor. The preacher must read and study to keep his mind in good trim. Above all, he must put heart work into his preaching. He must feel what he preaches. It must never be with him an easy thing to deliver a sermon. He must feel as if he could preach his very life away before the sermon is done.

> C. H. Spurgeon, *Metropolitan Tabernacle Pulpit*, Vol. 19, p. 462 [Psalm 39:3; Jeremiah 15:16]

Ignorance

The really wise . . . are too well instructed to be *ignorant* of their own *ignorance*.

C. H. Spurgeon, *Christ's Incarnation*, p. 98 [Matthew 2:2]

In the case of these wise men, we see *ignorance admitted.* Truly wise men are never above asking questions. . . . The knowledge of our *ignorance* is the doorstep of the temple of knowledge.

C. H. Spurgeon, *Christ's Incarnation*, p. 98 [Matthew 2:2]

Imposter

True Christians live for God, and work for God, and every one of us who claims to be a Christian is either working for God or else [is] an *imposter.* I repeat my declaration that the man who calls himself a Christian, and yet does nothing for Christ, is an *imposter.* He professes to be a fruit-bearing tree, yet he bears no fruit; he declares himself to be salt, yet he has no savour; he says that he is a light to the world, yet he never helps to remove its darkness by scattering his beams.

C. H. Spurgeon, *Spurgeon's Expository Encyclopedia*, Vol. 15, p. 272 [Psalm 90:17; Matthew 5:13–14]

Infirmities

Faith enables us so to rejoice in the Lord that our *infirmities* become platforms for the display of His grace.

C. H. Spurgeon, *An All-Round Ministry*, p. 16

Joy

A praiseful heart is a soul-winning heart. . . . A happy Christian attracts others by his *joy.*

C. H. Spurgeon, *Metropolitan Tabernacle Pulpit*, Vol. 36, p. 12 [Psalm 103:1]

To *enjoy* the love of God is paradise below the skies.

C. H. Spurgeon, *The Treasury of the Bible*, Vol. 7, p. 732
[Romans 5:5]

Perfect *joy* is the lily that springs from the root of God's manifested love "shed abroad in our hearts by the Holy Spirit."

C. H. Spurgeon [paraphrased], *Metropolitan Tabernacle Pulpit*, Vol. 32, p. 319 [Romans 5:5]

The more steadfastly we believe, the more . . . rapturous joy we shall experience.

C. H. Spurgeon, *Barbed Arrows*, p. 123

When the Lord cleanseth out the evil of our hearts . . . the oil of *joy* perfumes the soul.

C. H. Spurgeon, *Spurgeon's Expository Encyclopedia*, Vol. 10, p. 59 [Isaiah 61:3]

The *joy* which the gospel brings is not borrowed but blooms in its own garden.

C. H. Spurgeon, *Spurgeon's Expository Encyclopedia*, Vol. 10, p. 21 [Luke 2:10–12]

Although my *joy* is greater than most men, my depression is such as few have an idea of.

C. H. Spurgeon, *Metropolitan Tabernacle Pulpit*, Vol. 14, p. 188

The life of Luther might suffice to give a thousand instances, and he was by no means of the weaker sort. His great spirit was often in *seventh heaven of exultation,* and as frequently on the borders of despair.

C. H. Spurgeon, *Lectures to My Students*, p. 154

Fellowship with Christ is the fountain of *joy*. Other *joys* may help to fill it, but this fills of itself alone—up to the very brim, of fulness of *joy*.

> C. H. Spurgeon, *Spurgeon's Expository Encyclopedia*, Vol. 10,
> p. 48 [1 John 1:4]

Holy activity is the mother of holy *joy*. Growth in grace, too, is a fount of true *delight*. Never is a believer *happier* than when he grows in grace.

> C. H. Spurgeon, *Spurgeon's Expository Encyclopedia*, Vol. 10,
> p. 49 [1 John 1:4]

Faith made Abraham's trials blessings, and his inward *joy*, like Aaron's rod, swallowed up all the rods of his afflictions.

> C. H. Spurgeon, *Spurgeon's Expository Encyclopedia*, Vol. 10,
> p. 61 [Isaiah 61:3]

One hour with Christ is worth an eternity of all earth's *joys;* and communion with Him is the best, the surest, and the most ecstatic foretaste of the bliss of heaven.

> C. H. Spurgeon, *Gleanings Among the Sheaves*, p. 41

With His great infinite heart He loves me. It is a conquering thought; it utterly overcomes us and crushes us with its weight of *joy;* it bows us to the ground and casts us into a swoon of ecstasy.

> C. H. Spurgeon, *The Treasury of the Bible*, Vol. 7, p. 732

He who can live by faith shall have a constant supply of the oil of *joy* poured upon him by the Holy Spirit, and his mourning shall flee away.

> C. H. Spurgeon, *Spurgeon's Expository Encyclopedia*, Vol. 10,
> p. 61 [Isaiah 61:3]

The door of repentance opens into the halls of *Joy*.

> C. H. Spurgeon, *Barbed Arrows*, p. 224

Our *joys* begin and end with manifestations of Jesus' love!

C. H. Spurgeon, *Flowers From a Puritan's Garden*, p. 103
[John 14:21; John 17:13]

Wrapped in the beams of His love, as a dim star is eclipsed in the sunlight, so shall you sink into the sweet forgetfulness of *ecstasy*, which is the best description we can give of the *joys* of the redeemed.

C. H. Spurgeon, *The New Park Street Pulpit*, Vol. 4, p. 190
[John 17:24]

When our inward *joys* swell high, and burst into a song, then we hear preludes of the heavenly hallelujahs.

C. H. Spurgeon, *According to Promise*, p. 123 [1 Corinthians
2:9–10]

There is a quiet, rippling rill of intense comfort in a Christian's heart, even when he is cast down and tried, and at other times when trials are lightened there are cascades of delight, leaping cataracts of *joy*, whose silver spray is as pure as the flash of the fountains of Paradise. I know that there are many here who, like myself, understand what deep depression of spirit means, but yet we would not change our lot for all the mirth of fools or pomp of kings. . . . Amid the ashes of our pains live the sparks of our *joys*, ready to flame up when the breath of the Spirit sweetly blows thereon. Our latent *happiness* is a choicer heritage than the sinner's riotous glee.

C. H. Spurgeon, *The Treasury of the Bible*, Vol. 3, p. 53 [Psalm
119:54; John 17:24]

Why, if this Book said no more than "they shall be with Me where I am, that they may behold My glory," we should know enough of Heaven to make our hearts dance for *joy*. To be with Jesus where He is, to behold His glory, this is *bliss* pressed down and running over, more than our bosoms can hold.

C. H. Spurgeon, *The Treasury of the Bible*, Vol. 3, p. 55 [Psalm 119:54]

The communion table has been to many of us the palace of *delight.*

C. H. Spurgeon, *Spurgeon's Expository Encyclopedia*, Vol. 10, p. 63 [Isaiah 61:3]

Our *joy* is sadly diminished by our unbelief.

C. H. Spurgeon, *Metropolitan Tabernacle Pulpit*, Vol. 27, p. 81 [Galatians 5:22]

Have you ever seen the heavenly country? Has your eye ever been permitted to rest upon it? "No," says one, "certainly not." "Eye hath not seen, nor ear heard." "A very nice text, brother, go on with it; go on with it." You may make God say what He does not mean if you quote half a text. He says, "Eye hath not seen, nor ear heard, the things which God hath prepared for them that love Him; but God hath revealed them unto us by His Spirit." Hence we know these *joys* by revelation, and that is the best of knowledge. . . . He has revealed to us somewhat of the *joy* of communion with Christ; somewhat of the *joy* of conquered sin; somewhat of the *joy* of beholding His face, and praising and blessing His name.

C. H. Spurgeon, *The Treasury of the Bible*, pp. 55–56 [Psalm 119:54]

Christ being present with you, this is your main *joy. Enjoy* the feast for yourselves, or you will not be strong to hand out the living bread to others.

C. H. Spurgeon, *The Treasury of the Bible*, p. 353 [Song of Solomon 5:1]

What a *joy* to conquer yourself! What bliss to master your surroundings.

> C. H. Spurgeon, *The Treasury of the Bible*, Vol. 3, p. 85 [Psalm 119:162]

God's smile beheld by faith gives us fulness of *joy*.

> C. H. Spurgeon, *According to Promise*, pp. 30–31

Faith sees the clouds emptying themselves and making the little hills *rejoice* on every side.

> C. H. Spurgeon, *Faith's Checkbook*, p. 71 [Ecclesiastes 11:3]

The Holy Spirit is Himself a great portion of the inheritance of the saints. . . . He is everlasting life, and His gifts, graces, and workings are the first principles of *endless felicity*.

> C. H. Spurgeon, *According to Promise*, p. 121 [1 Corinthians 2:9–10; Romans 5:5]

A real *joy* of heavenly origin is ever with believers, and it is but the shadow of sorrow which falls upon them.

> C. H. Spurgeon, *Words of Wisdom for Daily Life*, p. 22

Holy fellowship brings heavenly *joy*.

> C. H. Spurgeon, *Spurgeon's Expository Encyclopedia*, Vol. 10, p. 63 [Isaiah 61:3]

Many a Christian has a thousand reasons for *joy* which he knows nothing of.

> C. H. Spurgeon, *Metropolitan Tabernacle Pulpit*, Vol. 27, p. 81 [Galatians 5:22]

Study the Word and ask for the teaching of the Spirit of God that you may understand it; so shall you discover *wells of delight*.

> C. H. Spurgeon, *Metropolitan Tabernacle Pulpit*, Vol. 27, 1881, p. 81 [Galatians 5:22; Jeremiah 15:16]

Joy is diminished . . . by walking at a distance from God. If you get away from the fire you will grow cold.

> C. H. Spurgeon, *Metropolitan Tabernacle Pulpit*, Vol. 27, p. 81
> [Galatians 5:22]

Joy is the center of a triplet, and you must have it so or not at all:—"Love, *joy*, peace."

> C. H. Spurgeon, *Metropolitan Tabernacle Pulpit*, Vol. 27, p. 82
> [Galatians 5:22]

Our heavenly Father *delights* in the *delight* of His children.

> C. H. Spurgeon, *Metropolitan Tabernacle Pulpit*, Vol. 27, p. 84
> [Galatians 5:22]

A drop of glory is sweet, but, oh, to taste a *joy* that is full of glory—is that possible here? Ay, and some of us bear witness that it is so: we have felt *joy* that we dare not tell, and could not tell if we dared: men would turn again and rend us, condemning us as utterly fanatical or out of our minds if we were to cast these pearls before them; but, oh, if they could guess what delicious draughts are held within the jewelled chalice of divine communion they would be ready to wade through hell itself to drink from it. Our *joy* is altogether unspeakable *joy* at times.

> C. H. Spurgeon, *Metropolitan Tabernacle Pulpit*, Vol. 27, p. 78
> [Galatians 5:22; 1 Peter 1:8; Jeremiah 15:16]

The Holy Spirit is the guarantee of everlasting *joy*.

> C. H. Spurgeon, *Metropolitan Tabernacle Pulpit*, Vol. 32,
> p. 323 [Romans 5:5; 15:13]

Confident hope breeds *inward joy*.

> C. H. Spurgeon, *Metropolitan Tabernacle Pulpit*, Vol. 32,
> p. 323 [Romans 5:5; 15:13]

Get to know and feel divine love, and the *fountains of delight* are unsealed to you—you are introduced to the *banquets of felicity.*

> C. H. Spurgeon, *Metropolitan Tabernacle Pulpit,* Vol. 32,
> p. 323 [Romans 5:5; 15:13]

Let us make worldlings know the fragrance of our *joyous hope.*

> C. H. Spurgeon, *Metropolitan Tabernacle Pulpit,* Vol. 32,
> p. 323 [Romans 5:5; 15:13; 2 Corinthians 2:14 (Moffatt)]

Let the sweet notes of your *happy life* charm others to Jesus! May the Lord cause you to spread abroad what He has shed abroad, and may that which perfumes your heart also perfume your house, your business, your conversation, and your whole life!

> C. H. Spurgeon, *Metropolitan Tabernacle Pulpit,* Vol. 32,
> p. 324 [Romans 5:5; 15:13; 2 Corinthians 2:14 (Moffatt)]

In our *present delight* in God we have the earnest of our endless *joy* in Him. . . . Oh, the love of God! The amazing, immeasurable, incomprehensible love of the Father! Oh, to feel this till our very souls are inflamed with it, and our unloving nature is all on fire with love to the great Lover of the souls of men!

> C. H. Spurgeon, *Metropolitan Tabernacle Pulpit,*Vol. 32,
> pp. 322–323 [Romans 5:5; 15:13]

Long for no *joy* but that which the Holy Spirit gives you.

> C. H. Spurgeon, *Spurgeon's Expository Encyclopedia,* Vol. 10,
> p. 60 [Isaiah 61:3; 1 John 1:1–4]

As perfume gives *delight* to the nostril, so the love of God, when shed abroad in the power of the Holy Spirit, imparts a singular sweetness to our emotions. . . . Meditate upon that love till you are ravished.

> C. H. Spurgeon, *Metropolitan Tabernacle Pulpit,* Vol. 32,
> p. 319 [Romans 5:5; 15:13; 2 Corinthians 2:14 (Moffatt)]

The oil of *joy* is poured out in . . . fellowship.

C. H. Spurgeon, *Spurgeon's Expository Encyclopedia*, Vol. 10,
p. 62 [Isaiah 61:3; 1 John 1:1–4]

He who knows the *joy* of the Lord will despise the *joy* of the world.

C. H. Spurgeon, *Spurgeon's Expository Encyclopedia*, Vol. 10,
p. 61 [Isaiah 61:3; 1 John 1:1–4]

He who has feasted at God's table, and had the oil of *joy* poured upon his head by the Holy Spirit, has risen above the fascinations of the hour.

C. H. Spurgeon, *Spurgeon's Expository Encyclopedia*, Vol. 10,
p. 61 [Isaiah 61:3; 1 John 1:1–4]

When the Holy Spirit comes and makes us . . . sensitive, then we . . . *rejoice* in the Lord; and the power of His might within us works in us a leaping of holy *joy*.

C. H. Spurgeon, *Spurgeon's Expository Encyclopedia*, Vol. 10,
p. 60 [Isaiah 61:3; 1 John 1:1–4]

Draw from the upper fountains, fill your pitcher at the eternal springs; ask neither for the cinnamon nor camphire of this world's gardens, but let your chief spices be the fruit of the Spirit, which are *joy* and peace through believing.

C. H. Spurgeon, *Spurgeon's Expository Encyclopedia*, Vol. 10,
p. 60 [Isaiah 61:3; 1 John 1:1–4; Romans 15:13]

How gloriously doth sacred *joy* lift us up above the sorrows of the world! Yea, more, how it lifts us up above earth's *joys!* The man who has once drunk the old wine of the kingdom does not desire the new and sour wine of earth.

C. H. Spurgeon, *Spurgeon's Expository Encyclopedia*, Vol. 10,
p. 61 [Isaiah 61:3; 1 John 1:1–4; Romans 15:13]

All the doctrines . . . when properly understood and received . . . foster Christian *joy*.

C. H. Spurgeon, *Spurgeon's Expository Encyclopedia*, Vol. 10,
p. 46 [1 John 1:4; Jeremiah 15:16]

The Lord . . . chose me . . . surely this ought to make us in our very worst and dullest moments sing for *joy*.

> C. H. Spurgeon, *Spurgeon's Expository Encyclopedia*, Vol. 10, p. 46 [1 John 1:4; Ephesians 1:4; 1 Peter 1:8]

Through faith in Christ's redemption every believer is "accepted in the Beloved," and stands in Jesus' righteousness, as fair in God's sight as if he had never sinned;—why, surely, here is a theme . . . for *overflowing joy!*

> C. H. Spurgeon, *Spurgeon's Expository Encyclopedia*, Vol. 10, p. 47 [1 John 1:4; Ephesians 1:6; 1 Peter 1:8]

If I were to so fill a glass with water that the gentlest touch would make it run over, that would be a picture of the *joy* the Christian sometimes has and should more constantly possess.

> C. H. Spurgeon, *Spurgeon's Expository Encyclopedia*, Vol. 10, p. 48 [1 John 1:4; Jeremiah 15:16; 1 Peter 1:8]

Search the Scriptures diligently, and your *joy* shall spread and deepen.

> C. H. Spurgeon, *Spurgeon's Expository Encyclopedia*, Vol. 10, p. 50 [1 John 1:4; Jeremiah 15:16; 1 Peter 1:8]

All the writings of Scripture, doctrinal, experimental, or practical, all have for their object, that which John declares in these words—"that your (our) *joy* may be full."

> C. H. Spurgeon, *Spurgeon's Expository Encyclopedia*, Vol. 10, p. 50 [1 John 1:4; Jeremiah 15:16; 1 Peter 1:8]

The root of faith produces the flower of *heart-joy*.

> C. H. Spurgeon, *Faith's Checkbook*, p. 65 [Psalm 33:21]

Faith must abide, though *joy* depart.

> C. H. Spurgeon, *Metropolitan Tabernacle Pulpit*, Vol. 28, p. 620 [1 Corinthians 13:13]

Justification

Though nowadays we hear of persons being healed before they have been wounded and brought into a certainty of *justification* without ever having lamented their condemnation, we are very dubious as to the value of such healings and *justifyings*. This style of things is not according to the truth. God never clothes men until He has first stripped them, nor does He quicken them by the gospel till first they are slain by the law. When you meet with persons in whom there is no trace of conviction of sin, you may be quite sure that they have not been wrought upon by the Holy Spirit, for "when He is come, He will reprove the world of sin, and of righteousness, and of judgment." Great care must be taken that faith is exercised upon Christ for a *complete salvation* and not for a part of it.

The Best of C. H. Spurgeon, p. 111

Knowledge

The *knowledge* of our ignorance is the doorstep of the temple of *knowledge*.

C. H. Spurgeon, *Christ's Incarnation*, p. 98

Law

Though nowadays we hear of persons being healed before they have been wounded and brought into a certainty of justification without ever having lamented their condemnation, we are very dubious as to the value of such healings and justifyings. This style of things is not according to the truth. God never clothes men until He has first stripped them, nor does He quicken them by the gospel till first they are slain by the *law*. When you meet with persons in whom there is no trace of conviction of sin, you may be quite sure that they have not been wrought upon by the Holy Spirit, for "when He is come, He will reprove the world of sin, and of righteousness, and of judgment." Great care must be taken that faith is exercised upon Christ for a complete salvation and not for a part of it.

The Best of C. H. Spurgeon, p. 111

The *law* is a storm which wrecks your hopes of self-salvation, but washes you upon the Rock of Ages.

C. H. Spurgeon, *The Best From All His Works*, p. 21

If we long to keep His statutes He will keep us; yea, His grace will keep us keeping His *law*.

C. H. Spurgeon, *The Best From All His Works*, p. 251

Light

As the dewdrop reflects the beam with which the great sun adorns it, so may we, in our measure, make the *light* of our great Father to sparkle before the eyes of men.

C. H. Spurgeon, *Words of Counsel for Christian Workers*, p. 90

Lone Wilderness

Christ chose this weapon [the Word] out of all the others, and used it in his earliest conflict, so, too, *He used it when no man was near.* The value of Holy Scripture is not alone seen in public teaching or striving for the truth; its still small voice is equally powerful when the servant of the Lord is enduring personal trial in the *lone wilderness.* The severest struggles of a true Christian are usually unknown to any but himself. Not in the family do we meet the most subtle temptations, but in the closet, not in the shop so much as in the recesses of our own spirit do we wrestle with principalities and powers. For these dread duels, "It is written" is the best sword and shield. Scripture to convince another man is good; but Scripture is most required to console, defend and sanctify our own soul.

> C. H. Spurgeon, *Spurgeon's Expository Encyclopedia*, Vol. 15, p. 222 [Matthew 4:4; Ephesians 6:17]

Lord, Lordship

Jesus must be received as *King* as well as Priest; and where there is any hesitancy about this, the foundation of godliness is not yet laid.

> *The Best of C. H. Spurgeon*, p. 114

If any man would be saved, he must believe that Jesus Christ is both *Lord* and *God*. Again, you must confess that Jesus Christ is *Lord,* that is, *Ruler* and *Master*. You must cheerfully become His disciple, follower, and servant. You must confess, "He is my *Master;* He is my *Lord.* I intend to be a soldier under Him. He shall be to me *Leader* and *Commander;* God has made Him such, and I accept Him as such." You are vocally to own Jesus; you are definitely and distinctly to say with your tongue, your mouth, your lips, that He is your *Lord* and *Saviour.* . . . With my mouth I do again confess the Lord Jesus, for I believe Him to be *very God of very God,* my *Master,* my *All*.

> C. H. Spurgeon, *Metropolitan Tabernacle Pulpit*, Vol. 32, pp. 247–248, 252 [Romans 10:9]

Love

True *love* is intense, its coals burn with vehement heat, it makes all things around it living.

> C. H. Spurgeon, *Seven Wonders of Grace*, p. 71

O, Saviour, accept these our poor praises. They come from those Thou *lovest.* . . . Oh, we can say we *love* thee; we wish we *loved* Thee more; but Thou art very dear to us. There is nought on earth like Thee. For the *love* of Thy name

we would live and die. If we think we *love* Thee more than
we do, we pray that we may yet *love* Thee more than we
think. Oh, take these hearts right away and unite them with
Thine own, and be Thou heart and soul and life and everything to us; for whom have we in Heaven but Thee, and
there is none upon earth we desire beside Thee.

C. H. Spurgeon, *C. H. Spurgeon's Prayers*, pp. 8–9 [Psalm
73:25]

Faith is an act of the understanding; but it also proceeds
from the heart. God gives salvation to faith because it resides next door to the affections, and is near akin to *love;*
and *love* is the parent and the nurse of every holy feeling
and act. *Love* to God is obedience, *love* to God is holiness.
To *love* God and to *love* man is to be conformed to the image
of Christ; and this is salvation.

C. H. Spurgeon, *All of Grace*, p. 62 [Romans 10:9; John 14:21]

We can see the reflection of a soul's *love* in its most passionate utterances.

C. H. Spurgeon, *Seven Wonders of Grace*, p. 73

Words have no power to bear the weight of meaning
which lies in *love* to Christ. O how she *loved!* Her eyes, her
hair, her tears, herself, she counted all as nothing for His
dear sake: words failed her as they fail us, and therefore she
betook herself to deeds in order to let her heart have vent.
Alabaster box and ointment were all too little for Him, the
essence of her heart was distilled to bathe His feet, and the
glory of her head was unbound to furnish Him with a towel.
He was her Lord, her all in all.

C. H. Spurgeon, *Seven Wonders of Grace*, 1   9595p. 67 [Luke
7:37–38]

Love to God will induce meditation. Neglect of meditation argues want of *love*.

> C. H. Spurgeon, *The Treasury of David*, Vol. 3, p. 443 [Psalm 119:97]

The *love* which the early Christians felt toward the Lord . . . was a passion with them of such a vehement and all-consuming energy, that it was visible in their actions, spoke in their common talk, and looked out of their eyes even in their commonest glances. *Love* to Jesus was a flame which fed upon the core and heart of their being; and, therefore, from its own force burned its way into the outer man, and shone there.

> C. H. Spurgeon, *Day by Day with C. H. Spurgeon*, Compiled by Al Bryant, p. 254 [1 John 5:1–3]

Do you know, O saint, how much the Lord *loves* you? Can you measure His *love?* Do you know how great is the affection of His soul toward you? Go measure heaven with a span; go weigh the mountain in the scales; go take the ocean's water, and tell each drop; go count the sand upon the sea's wide shore; and when you have accomplished this, you will be able to tell how much He *loves* you.

> C. H. Spurgeon, *Day by Day with C. H. Spurgeon*, Compiled by Al Bryant, p. 215 [Ephesians 3:17–19]

Let your memory treasure up everything about Christ which you have either felt, or known, or believed, and then let your fond *affections* hold Him fast forevermore. *Love* the person of your Lord! Bring forth the alabaster box of your heart, even though it be broken, and let all the precious ointment of your *affection* come streaming on His pierced feet.

> C. H. Spurgeon, *Day by Day with C. H. Spurgeon*, Compiled by Al Bryant, p. 154 [Luke 24:29]

Oh! there are times when we are as full of heaven as we can hold this side of the Jordan, and when we know Christ's *love* because He kisses us "with the kisses of His mouth," and we drink deep draughts of His *love*.

C. H. Spurgeon, *Spurgeon's Expository Encyclopedia*, p. 388

In our present delight in God we have the earnest of our endless joy in Him. . . . Oh, the *love* of God! The *amazing, immeasurable, incomprehensible love* of the Father! Oh, to feel this till our very souls are inflamed with it, and our un-loving nature is all on fire with *love* to the great *Lover* of the souls of men!

C. H. Spurgeon, *Metropolitan Tabernacle Pulpit*, Vol. 32,
pp. 322–323 [Romans 5:5, 15:13]

Love . . . is as sure in the night of darkness as in the brightness of the day of joy.

C. H. Spurgeon, *Day by Day with C. H. Spurgeon*, Compiled by
Al Bryant, p. 237 [Hebrews 10:24]

To hear of the *love* of God is sweet—to believe it most precious—but to enjoy it is paradise below the skies.

C. H. Spurgeon, *The Treasury of the Bible*, Vol. 7, p. 732
[2 Thessalonians 2:16–17]

With His great infinite heart He *loves* me. It is a conquer-ing thought; it utterly overcomes us and crushes us with its weight of joy; it bows us to the ground and casts us into a swoon of ecstasy.

C. H. Spurgeon, *The Treasury of the Bible*, Vol. 7, p. 732

The *love* of God is that fountain from which all the rivers of mercy which have ever gladdened our race—all the riv-ers of grace in time and glory hereafter—take their rise.

C. H. Spurgeon, *The Treasury of the Bible*, Vol. 7, p. 734

This is the holy reasoning of *love;* it draws no license from grace, but rather *feels the strong constraints of gratitude leading it to holiness.*

> C. H. Spurgeon, *The Treasury of the Bible,* Vol. 7, p. 736

Love presides over the arrangements of grace and strikes upon the bell when the best moment has arrived. God blesses us by His temporary delays, as well as by His prompt replies.

> C. H. Spurgeon, *According to Promise,* p. 116 [Acts 7:17; John 11:5–6]

Love closes the hand of divine bounty, and restrains the outflow of favour, when it sees that a solid gain will ensue from a period of trial. . . . The time of the promise corresponds with the time most enriching to heart and soul.

> C. H. Spurgeon, *According to Promise,* pp. 116–117 [Acts 7:17; John 11:5–6]

The Father has not only resolved to enrich us in the future, but even now He has endowed us with the treasures of His *love.*

> C. H. Spurgeon, *According to Promise,* p. 119 [Ephesians 1:13–14]

Marriage

Sometimes we have seen a model *marriage,* founded on pure love, and cemented in mutual esteem. Therein, the husband acts as a tender head; and the wife, as a true spouse, realizes the model marriage-relation, and sets forth what our oneness with the Lord ought to be. She delights in her husband, in his person, his character, his affection; to her, he is not only the chief and foremost of mankind, but in her eyes he is all-in-all; her heart's love belongs to him, and to him only. She finds sweetest content and solace in his company, his fellowship, his fondness; he is her little world, her Paradise, her choice treasure. At any time, she would gladly lay aside her own pleasure to find it doubled in gratifying him. She is glad to sink her individuality in his. She seeks no renown for herself; his honour is reflected upon her, and she rejoices in it. She would defend his name with her dying breath; safe enough is he where she can speak for him. The domestic circle is her kingdom; that she may there create happiness and comfort, is her life-work; and his smiling gratitude is all the reward she seeks. Even in her dress, she thinks of him; without constraint she consults his taste, and considers nothing beautiful which is distasteful to him. A tear from his eye, because of any unkindness on her part would grievously torment her. She asks not how her behaviour may please a stranger, or how another's judgment may approve her conduct; let her beloved be content, and she is glad. He has many objects in life, some of which she does not quite understand; but she believes in them all, and anything that she can do to promote them, she delights to perform. He lavishes love on her, and, in return, she lavishes love on him. Their object in life is common. There are points where their affections so intimately unite that none could tell which is first and which is second. . . .

Happy woman and happy man! If heaven be found on earth, they have it! At last, the two are so blended, so engrafted on one stem, that their old age presents a lovely attachment, a common sympathy, by which its infirmities are greatly alleviated, and its burdens are transformed into fresh bonds of love. So happy a union of will, sentiment, thought, and heart exists between them, that the two streams of their life have washed away the dividing bank, and run on as one broad current of united existence till their common joy falls into the ocean of eternal felicity.

> C. H. Spurgeon, *C. H. Spurgeon Autobiography*, Vol. 1, "The Early Years," p. 410

It was ever the settled purpose of my married life that I should never hinder him *[Charles Spurgeon]* in his work for the Lord, never try to keep him from fulfilling his engagements, never plead my own ill-health as a reason why he should remain at home with me. I thank God, now, that He enabled me to carry out this determination, and rejoice that I have no cause to reproach myself with being a drag on the swift wheels of his consecrated life.

> Mrs. C. H. Spurgeon, *C. H. Spurgeon Autobiography*, Vol. 1, "The Early Years," p. 289

Meditation (Contemplation)

Without *meditation* reading is a waste of time and an indignity offered to the Word.

> C. H. Spurgeon, *The Treasury of David*, Vol. 3, p. 473 [Psalm 119:148]

If you would excel in heavenly wisdom, and hallow your life, abundantly occupy yourself with sacred *meditation.*

> C. H. Spurgeon, *The Treasury of David*, Vol. 3, p. 443 [Psalm 119]

Meditation extracts sweetness from the promises.

> C. H. Spurgeon, *The Treasury of David*, Vol. 3, p. 473 [Psalm 119:148]

The way to spiritual health is to exercise one's self in holy *contemplation.*

> C. H. Spurgeon, *Devotions and Prayers of C. H. Spurgeon*, p. 7 of Preface

No spiritual exercise is more profitable to the soul than that of devout *meditation;* why are many of us so exceeding slack in it?

> C. H. Spurgeon, *The Treasury of David*, Vol. 3, p. 161 [Psalm 119:15]

Faith gathers the handfuls of sacred corn from which *contemplation* threshes out the ears and prepares soul-sustaining bread.

> *The Best of C. H. Spurgeon*, p. 38

Love to God will induce *meditation*. Neglect of *meditation* argues want of love.

> C. H. Spurgeon, *The Treasury of David*, Vol. 3, p. 443 [Psalm 119:97]

Meditation and careful thought exercise us and strengthen the soul for the reception of the yet more lofty truths. . . . Our Lord wishes us to be good slingers, and he puts up some precious truth in a lofty place where we cannot get it down except by slinging at it; and, at last, we hit the mark and find food for our souls. Then have we the double benefit of learning the art of *meditation* and partaking of the sweet truth which it has brought within our reach. We must *meditate*, brothers. These grapes will yield no wine till we tread upon them. These olives must be put under the wheel, and pressed again and again, that the oil may flow therefrom.

> C. H. Spurgeon, *Spurgeon's Expository Encyclopedia*, Vol. 15, p. 211

"I will delight myself in thy statutes." In this verse delight follows *meditation*, of which it is the true flower and outgrowth. When we have no other solace, but are quite alone, it will be a glad thing for the heart to turn upon itself, and sweetly whisper, "I will delight myself. What if no minstrel sings in the hall, I will delight myself. If the time of the singing of birds has not yet arrived, and the voice of the turtle is not heard in our land, yet I will delight myself." This is the choicest and noblest of all rejoicing; in fact, it is the good part which can never be taken from us; but there is no delighting ourselves with anything below that which God intended to be the soul's eternal satisfaction. . . . When the believer once peruses the sacred pages his soul burns within him as he turns first to one and then to another of the royal words of the great King, words full and firm, immutable and divine.

> C. H. Spurgeon, *The Treasury of David*, Vol. 3, Pt. 1, p. 161
> [Psalm 119:16; Jeremiah 15:16]

True fathers in grace *meditate* upon Christ; they feed upon Scripture, press the juice of it, and inwardly enjoy the flavor of it.

> C. H. Spurgeon

Memory

This is the true art of *memory*, to cause them to delight in what they learn. Such instructions as we take in with sweetness, they stick with us, and run in our minds night and day.

> C. H. Spurgeon (quoting Thomas Manton), *The Treasury of David*, Vol. 3, Pt. 1, p. 161 [Psalm 119:16]

Mercy

He will not allow His *mercies* to become veils to hide his face from the eyes of our love; but He makes them windows through which He looks upon us. The Promiser is seen in the promise, and we watch to see His hand in the performance.

> C. H. Spurgeon, *According to Promise*, p. 57

Delay has produced the patience of hope, and made every *mercy* to wear a double value.

> C. H. Spurgeon, *According to Promise*, p. 57

Faith occupies the position of a channel or conduit-pipe. Grace is the fountain and the stream: faith is the aqueduct along which the flood of *mercy* flows down to refresh the thirsty sons of men.

> C. H. Spurgeon, *Metropolitan Tabernacle Pulpit,* Vol. 27,
> p. 401 [Ephesians 2:8]

Mind

When filled with holy truth the *mind* rests.

> Author unknown, probably C. H. Spurgeon

Ministers

Christ's *ministers* are your souls' physicians. We are not fiddlers to tickle your ears, nor confectioners to please your palates, but physicians to cure your diseases; and if you nauseate our most needful medicines we dare not withhold them, and gratify you with sugared poisons.

> C. H. Spurgeon (quoting Daniel Burgess), *Eccentric Preachers,*
> p. 122

It is sadly common among *ministers* to add a word or subtract a word from the passage, or in some way to debase the language of sacred writ. Believers in verbal inspiration should be studiously careful to be verbally correct. Let us quote the words as they stand in the best possible translation, and it will be better still if we know the original, and can tell if our version fails to give the sense. How much mischief may arise out of an accidental alteration of the Word!

> The Greatest Fight in the World, C. H. Spurgeon's "Final
> Manifesto," p. 23

Need

He who has most grace is most conscious of his *need* of more grace.

> C. H. Spurgeon, *Metropolitan Tabernacle Pulpit,* Vol. 29,
> p. 454 [Romans 6:14–15]

Obedience

Obedience is faith incarnate.

C. H. Spurgeon, *My Sermon Notes*, Vol. 4, p. 215

Faith is an act of the understanding; but it also proceeds from the heart. God gives salvation to faith because it resides next door to the affections, and is near akin to love; and love is the parent and the nurse of every holy feeling and act. Love to God is *obedience*, love to God is holiness. To love God and to love man is to be conformed to the image of Christ; and this is salvation.

C. H. Spurgeon, *All of Grace*, p. 62 [Romans 10:9; John 14:21]

To come to Jesus, not only implies leaving all other confidences, and trusting Christ, it also means following Him. If you trust Him, you must *obey* Him. If you leave your soul in His hands, you must take Him to be your Master, and your Lord, as well as your Saviour. Christ has come to save you from sin, not in sin. He will make you holy.

C. H. Spurgeon, *Metropolitan Tabernacle Pulpit*, Sermon No. 2,349, p. 87 [John 6:37]

You must take Jesus to be your sole confidence, and then you must be *obedient* to His command, and take Him to be your master, and Lord. Will you do that? If not, I have nothing to say to you except this,—he that believeth not in Him will perish without hope.

C. H. Spurgeon, *Metropolitan Tabernacle Pulpit*, Sermon No. 2,349, p. 87 [John 6:37]

Pain, Poverty

Faith about my *pain*, my *poverty*, my despondency, my old age—that is faith.

C. H. Spurgeon, *Metropolitan Tabernacle Pulpit*, Vol. 27, p. 643 [Psalm 73:28]

Passion

Oh, to *burn* in our secret heart while we *blaze* before the eyes of others! This is the work of the Spirit of God. Work it in us, O adorable Comforter!

C. H. Spurgeon, *Lectures to My Students*, p. 193

Patience

Patience is a pearl which is only found in the deep seas of affliction; and only grace can find it there, bring it to the surface, and adorn the neck of faith therewith.

C. H. Spurgeon, *Metropolitan Tabernacle Pulpit*, Vol. 32, p. 314

Plead(ing)

It is well to be *pleading* evermore with God.

C. H. Spurgeon, *Lectures to My Students*, p. 316

Plead and persuade, even to tears—brethren, we must *plead*.

C. H. Spurgeon, *Lectures to My Students*, p. 342

Mention your own experience—and *plead* with men to come and taste the same.

C. H. Spurgeon, *Lectures to My Students*, p. 342

We win hearts for Jesus by love,—by *pleading* with God for them—(and) by *pleading* with them for God.

C. H. Spurgeon, *The Soul Winner*, p. 238

We are commissioned to *plead* for Christ, even as He is commissioned to *plead* for us.

C. H. Spurgeon, *An All-Round Ministry*, p. 380 [John 20:21]

Plead with God: *plead* with God: *plead* with God! That praying is poor shift that is not made up of *pleading.* "Bring forth your reasons," saith the Lord. Bring forth your strong arguments. O, what prayers were those of John Knox, when he seemed to say to God, "Save Scotland for this reason—for that reason—for another reason—for yet one more reason,"—the number of his motives still multiplying with the fervour of his heart. So did he labour with God as though he *pleaded* for his life, and would not let Him go until he had gained his suit for Scotland.

> C. H. Spurgeon, *Spurgeon's Expository Encyclopedia*, Vol. 15, p. 437 [2 Corinthians 5:20–21]

Let us seek grace to become importunate *pleaders* of a sort that cannot be denied, since their faith overcomes Heaven by prayer.

> C. H. Spurgeon, *The Treasury of the Bible*, Vol. 6, p. 73 [Luke 18:8; 2 Corinthians 5:20–21]

Praise

O, Saviour, accept these our poor *praises*. They come from those Thou lovest. . . . Oh, we can say we love Thee; we wish we loved Thee more; but Thou art very dear to us. There is nought on earth like Thee. For the love of Thy name we would live and die. If we think we love Thee more than we do, we pray that we may yet love Thee more than we think. Oh take these hearts right away and unite them with Thine own, and be Thou heart and soul and life and everything to us; for whom have we in Heaven but Thee, and there is none upon earth we desire beside Thee.

> C. H. Spurgeon, *C. H. Spurgeon's Prayers*, pp. 8–9 [Psalm 73:25]

Lord . . . We know not how abundantly enough to utter the memory of Thy great goodness. We would make our *praises* equal to our expectations, and our expectations equal to Thy promises.

> C. H. Spurgeon, *C. H. Spurgeon's Prayers*, p. 80

From prayer to *praise* is never a long or difficult journey.

Charles Spurgeon: The Best From All His Works

He is a triune God: render Him triune *praise.* Bless Him; bless Him; bless Him; be always blessing Him.

C. H. Spurgeon, *Metropolitan Tabernacle Pulpit*, Vol. 36, p. 8
[Psalm 103:1]

Praise is the alpha and the omega of a Christian life. *Praise* is the life of life. . . . One streak of sparkling crystal should run through the entire mass of life—and that should be *praise* unto God.

C. H. Spurgeon, *Metropolitan Tabernacle Pulpit*, Vol. 36, p. 1
[Psalm 103:1]

Praise is the rehearsal of our eternal song. By grace we learn to sing, and in glory we continue to sing.

C. H. Spurgeon, *Metropolitan Tabernacle Pulpit*, Vol. 36, p. 12
[Psalm 103:1]

A *praiseful* heart is a soul-winning heart. . . . A happy Christian attracts others by his joy.

C. H. Spurgeon, *Metropolitan Tabernacle Pulpit*, Vol. 36, p. 12
[Psalm 103:1]

Prayer

Especially is it the Holy Spirit's work to maintain in us a devotional frame of mind whilst we are discoursing. This is a condition to be greatly coveted—to continue *praying* while you are occupied with preaching . . . to keep the eye on the throne, and the wing in perpetual motion. . . . Oh, to *burn in our secret heart* while we blaze before the eyes of others! This is the work of the Spirit of God. Work it in us, O adorable Comforter!

C. H. Spurgeon, *Lectures to My Students*, p. 193

Spurgeon said, *"Prayer* is the forerunner of mercy."

John MacArthur, *The MacArthur New Testament Commentary,*
Matthew 1–7, p. 347 [Matthew 5:43–48]

A groan cometh not from the lips, but from the heart. A groan then is a part of *prayer* which we owe to the Holy Ghost, and the same is true of all the *prayer* which wells up from the deep fountains of our inner life. The prophet cried, ". . . I am pained at my very heart: my heart maketh a noise in me." This deep groundswell of desire, this tidal motion of the life-floods is caused by the Holy Spirit. His work is never superficial, but always deep and inward.

C. H. Spurgeon, *Metropolitan Tabernacle Pulpit,* Vol. 26,
p. 223 [Romans 8:26–27; Psalm 38:9; Jeremiah 4:19]

Frequently the richest answers are not the speediest. . . . A *prayer* may be all the longer on its voyage because it is bringing us a heavier freight of blessing. Delayed answers are not only trials of faith, but they give us an opportunity of honouring God by our steadfast confidence in Him under apparent repulses.

C. H. Spurgeon, *Flowers From a Puritan's Garden,* p. 266
[Habakkuk 2:3]

When in *prayer* for the great congregation at the Tabernacle, I have been so lifted up that, whether in the body or out of the body, I could not tell, and I have just lost myself in a rapture of adoring ecstasy before the throne of God. But there has been equal joy in fellowship with two or three kindred spirits with Jesus in the midst, or in communion alone with God at the mercy seat.

C. H. Spurgeon, *Spurgeon's Sermons Preached on Unusual*
Occasions, pp. 272–273 [2 Corinthians 12:2–5]

Beloved, what a different view of *prayer* God has from that which men think to be the correct one. . . . To Him fine language is as sounding brass or a tinkling cymbal, but a groan has music in it.

> C. H. Spurgeon, *Metropolitan Tabernacle Pulpit,* Vol. 26, p. 223

To *pray* over the Word, brings us great joy as we continue to make fresh discoveries of the heights, and depths, and lengths, and breadths of the love of Christ, and as we find new meanings in texts that have long been familiar to us.

> C. H. Spurgeon, *Spurgeon's Sermons Preached on Unusual Occasions,* p. 273 [Ephesians 3:18–19]

The preparation for the Christian ministry should be one of the best means of grace that a man can have, and . . . *prayer* especially should be to him a constant joy and delight.

> C. H. Spurgeon, *Spurgeon's Sermons Preached on Unusual Occasions,* p. 273 [Psalm 37:4]

Prayer is one of the necessary wheels of the machinery of providence.

> C. H. Spurgeon, *Spurgeon's Sermons Preached on Unusual Occasions,* p. 24 [Philippians 4:6]

True *prayer* is true *power.*

> C. H. Spurgeon, *Spurgeon's Sermons Preached on Unusual Occasions,* p. 25 [John 14:12–14]

Some brethren *pray* by the yard; but true *prayer* is measured by weight, and not by length.

> C. H. Spurgeon

From *prayer* to praise is never a long or difficult journey.

> *Charles Spurgeon: The Best From All His Works*

The tail feathers of pride should be pulled out of our *prayers,* for they need only the wing feathers of faith.

> C. H. Spurgeon, *Metropolitan Tabernacle Pulpit,* Vol. 26, p. 224 [Romans 8:26–27]

Prayers

Great God . . . We long that false doctrine may fly like birds of darkness before the light of Thy coming.

C. H. Spurgeon, *C. H. Spurgeon's Prayers*, p. 68

We do with all our hearts pray "Thy kingdom come, Thy will be done on earth, as it is in heaven." Lord, help us to do Thy will. Take the crippled kingdom of our manhood and reign Thou over it. Let spirit and body be consecrated to God. May there be no reserves; may everything be given up to Thee. Reign for ever! Pierced King despised and nailed to a tree, sit Thou on the glorious high throne in our hearts, and may our lives prove that Thou art Lord over us; by our every thought and desire, and imagination, and word, and act, in every respect being under Thy divine control.

C. H. Spurgeon, *C. H. Spurgeon's Prayers*, pp. 68–69

And now, Father, glorify Thy Son! In scattering pardons through His precious blood glorify Thy Son! In sending forth the Eternal Spirit to convince men and bring them to His feet, Father, glorify Thy Son! In enriching Thy saints with gifts and graces, and building them up into His image, Father, glorify Thy Son! In the gathering together of the whole company of His elect and in the hastening of His kingdom and His coming, Father, glorify Thy Son! Beyond this prayer we cannot go: "Glorify Thy Son that Thy Son also may glorify Thee," and unto Father, Son, and Holy Spirit be glory for ever and ever. Amen.

C. H. Spurgeon, *C. H. Spurgeon's Prayers*, p. 152 [John 17:1]

O, my blessed Master, help me I pray Thee to keep the mirror of my mind in the right position, that evermore I may see Thee. True, it will be but as in a glass darkly, but even that will be a marvelous preparation for beholding Thee face to face.

C. H. Spurgeon, *Flowers From a Puritan's Garden*, p. 268

My God, grant me grace ever to put the first first, and the last last. Let me . . . reckon that gain to be loss which is gained by loss of communion with Thee, and that profit to be unprofitable which renders me less profitable to Thee.

C. H. Spurgeon, *Flowers From a Puritan's Garden*, p. 261

O Lord . . . Let us gaze upon Thy glory till we are transformed by the sight, and become Christ-like among the sons of men.

C. H. Spurgeon, *C. H. Spurgeon's Prayers*, p. 76

Lord, restore to Thy Church the love of strong doctrine. May Thy truth yet prevail. Purge out from among Thy Church those who would lead others away from the truth. . . . May we live to see Thy Church shine forth clear as the sun and fair as the moon, and terrible as an army with banners.

C. H. Spurgeon, *C. H. Spurgeon's Prayers*, p. 82

Lord . . . We pray that we may be men of prayer, taken up with it, that it may take us up and bear us as on its wings towards Heaven.

C. H. Spurgeon, *C. H. Spurgeon's Prayers*, p. 73

Lord . . . We know not how abundantly enough to utter the memory of Thy great goodness. We would make our praises equal to our expectations, and our expectations equal to Thy promises.

C. H. Spurgeon, *C. H. Spurgeon's Prayers*, p. 80

Come, Holy Spirit, we do know Thee; Thou hast often overshadowed us. Come, more fully take possession of us. Standing now as we feel we are right up at the mercy seat our very highest prayer is for perfect holiness, complete consecration, entire cleansing from every evil. Take our heart, our head, our hands, our feet, and use us all for Thee. Lord, take our substance. . . . Take our talent. . . . Let every gain of mental attainment be still that we may serve Thee better.

> C. H. Spurgeon, *C. H. Spurgeon's Prayers*, pp. 3–4 [Psalm 46:10; 36:7; 92:1, 4]

O Lord God, help us now really to worship Thee. . . . Enable us to rise clean out of this world. May we get rid of all its down-dragging tendencies. May the attractions of these grosser things be gone, and do Thou catch us away to Thyself. We do not ask to be entranced nor to see an angel in shining apparel, but we do ask that by faith we may see Jesus, and may His presence be so evidently realized among us that we may rejoice as well as if our eyes beheld Him.

> C. H. Spurgeon, *C. H. Spurgeon's Prayers*, p. 7 [Hebrews 12:2; 3:1]

O, Thou precious Lord Jesus Christ, we do adore Thee with all our hearts. Thou art Lord of all. We bless Thee for becoming man. . . . Thou hast ransomed Thy people with Thy heart's blood. Be Thou, therefore, for ever beloved and adored. And now . . . Thou art risen. Our souls would track the shining way by which Thou hast ascended through the gate of pearl up to Thy Father's Throne.

> C. H. Spurgeon, *C. H. Spurgeon's Prayers*, pp. 7–8 [Acts 1:9]

Come, Holy Spirit, help us to feel that we are in the immediate presence of God; and may this thought lead us to sincere and earnest petitioning.

> C. H. Spurgeon, *C. H. Spurgeon's Prayers*, p. 135 [Romans 8:26]

Lord, sanctify us. Oh! that Thy Spirit might come and saturate every faculty, subdue every passion, and use every power of our nature for obedience to God.

> C. H. Spurgeon, *C. H. Spurgeon's Prayers*, p. 3 [John 17:17]

Most blessed Lord, look down upon those who do not love Thee. O Redeemer, look upon them with those eyes of Thine which are as flames of fire. Let them see how ill they treat Thee. May they consider within themselves how dire is the ingratitude which can be negligent of a Saviour's blood.

> C. H. Spurgeon, *C. H. Spurgeon's Prayers*, p. 9 [Revelation 1:14; 2:18]

O God, we praise Thee for keeping us. . . . Blessed be the Lord for every office sustained by each divine person, and for the divine blessing which has come streaming down to us through each one of those condescending titles worn by the Father, Son, and the Holy Spirit.

> C. H. Spurgeon, *C. H. Spurgeon's Prayers*, p. 14 [Jude 24–25; 2 Corinthians 13:14]

Lord, forgive us all our sin. May Thy pardoned ones have a renewed sense of their acceptance in the Beloved. If any cloud has arisen to hide Thee from any believing eye, take that cloud away.

> C. H. Spurgeon, *C. H. Spurgeon's Prayers*, p. 15 [1 John 1:7–9; Ephesians 1:6]

Lord, save men, gather out the company of the redeemed people; let those whom the Father gave to Christ be brought out from among the ruins of the fall to be His joy and crown.

> C. H. Spurgeon, *C. H. Spurgeon's Prayers*, p. 17 [John 6:37; Philippians 4:1]

Lord, keep us right, true in doctrine, true in experience, true in life, true in word, true in deed. Let us have an intense agony of spirit concerning the many who are going

113

down to the everlasting fire of which our Master spoke. Lord, save them! LORD, SAVE THEM!

> C. H. Spurgeon, *C. H. Spurgeon's Prayers*, p. 17 [Luke 19:10]

There are some that we love in the flesh who have not yet decided for God. Behold it trembles in the balance! Cast in Thy cross, O Jesus, and turn the scale! Oh! Love irresistible, come forth, and carry by blessed storm the hearts which have not yet yielded to the attacks of the law! Oh! that some who never could be melted, even by the furnace of Sinai, may be dissolved by the beams of love from the tearful eyes of Jesus.

> C. H. Spurgeon, *C. H. Spurgeon's Prayers*, p. 22 [Matthew 23:37]

The Lord pour out His Spirit upon us that every chamber of our nature may be sweetened and perfumed with the indwelling of God, till our imagination shall only delight in things chaste and pure; till our memory shall cast out the vile stuff from the dark chambers; till we shall expect and long for heavenly things, and our treasure shall all be in heaven and our heart be there. Take our highest manhood, Lord, and saturate it in Thy love, till like Gideon's fleece it is filled with dew, every lock and every single fleck of it, not a single portion of it left unmoistened by the dew from heaven.

> C. H. Spurgeon, *C. H. Spurgeon's Prayers*, pp. 57–58
> [Philippians 4:8; Ephesians 5:18–19]

O, Saviour, let Thy Kingdom come. . . . O that Thou wouldst hear creation's groans and come quickly. O Thou great Deliverer, joy of the earth art Thou, the expected of the tribes of Israel still; come, we beseech Thee, Thou absent love, Thou dear unknown, Thou fairest of ten thousand fair; come a second time to earth and to the sons of men, and specially to Thy Bride, the Church. Even so come quickly, Lord Jesus. Amen.

> C. H. Spurgeon, *C. H. Spurgeon's Prayers*, p. 99 [Romans 8:22; Revelation 22:20]

Our Father, which art in heaven, hallowed be Thy name. . . . With heart and mind, and memory and fear, and hope and joy, we worship the Most High. . . . With lowliest reverence, with truest love, we worship God in Christ Jesus, uniting therewith with all the redeemed host above, with angels and principalities and powers.

> C. H. Spurgeon, *C. H. Spurgeon's Prayers*, p. 67 [Matthew 6:9]

We thank Thee, Lord, for every leaf of the Book, not only for its promises which are inexpressibly sweet, but for its precepts in which our soul delights, and especially for the revelation of Thy Son, our Lord and Saviour Jesus Christ. O God, we thank Thee for the manifestation of Him even in the types and shadows of the Old Testament. These are inexpressibly glorious to us, full of wondrous value, inexpressibly dear because in them and through them we see the Lord.

> C. H. Spurgeon, *C. H. Spurgeon's Prayers*, p. 123

O, Saviour, accept these our poor praises. They come from those Thou lovest. . . . Oh, we can say we love Thee; we wish we loved Thee more; but Thou art very dear to us. There is nought on earth like Thee. For the love of Thy name we would live and die. If we think we love Thee more than we do, we pray that we may yet love Thee more than we think. Oh take these hearts right away and unite them with Thine own, and be Thou heart and soul and life and everything to us; for whom have we in Heaven but Thee, and there is none upon earth we desire beside Thee.

> C. H. Spurgeon, *C. H. Spurgeon's Prayers*, pp. 8–9 [Psalm 73:25]

Sanctify us to Thy service, and hold us to it. Comfort us with Thy presence; elevate us into Thy presence. Make us like Thyself; bring us near Thyself, and in all things glorify Thyself in us, whether we live or die.

Bless the poor, remember the needy among Thine own people; help and succour them. Bless the sick, and be very near the dying. . . . Thy kingdom come not here only, but in every land and nation. Lands across the flood remember with plenitude of Thy grace. Let the whole earth be filled with Thy Glory.

> C. H. Spurgeon, *C. H. Spurgeon's Prayers*, p. 139 [Isaiah 6:3; 2 Corinthians 3:18, Amplified Bible]

O blessed hand of Jesus, drive in the nail of divine love! Smite hard, Lord. Force out the rusted iron of my selfishness. Let not a fragment of it remain. Love alone can vanquish love. Thyself alone can conquer self in me. No secondary force will suffice. My God, Thou must display Thy Godhead's power of love, or my vile heart will never part with self.

> C. H. Spurgeon, *Flowers From a Puritan's Garden*, p. 105

Lord, give us grace to climb to this seventh beatitude! Purify our minds that we may be "first pure, then peaceable," and fortify our souls, that our peaceableness may not lead us into cowardice and despair, when for Thy sake we are persecuted.

> C. H. Spurgeon, *Morning and Evening*, p. 155 [Matthew 5:8–12; Hebrews 7:2]

Lord, do use us for Thy glory. Shine upon us, O Emmanuel, that we may reflect Thy brightness; dwell in us, O Jesus, that out of us may come the power of Thy life. Make Thy Church to work miracles, because the miracle-worker is in the midst of her. Oh! send us times of revival, seasons of great refreshing; and then times of aggression, when the army of the Lord of Hosts shall push its way into the very centre of the adversary, and overthrow the foe in the name of the King of Kings.

C. H. Spurgeon, *C. H. Spurgeon's Prayers*, p. 138
[2 Corinthians 4:6; 3:18 Amplified Bible]

O my Lord, whatever others may think of me, let me be more and more sensible of Thy presence, and of the glorious privileges and hopes which are created in the heart by Thy grace! If men should even say of me, as of Joseph, "Behold, this dreamer cometh," it will not grieve me so long as Thou art with me, and Thy favor makes me blest.

C. H. Spurgeon, *Flowers From a Puritan's Garden*, p. 106
[Genesis 37:19]

Lord . . . May Thy Word be the supreme ruler of our being. May we give ourselves up to its sacred law to be obedient to its every hint, wishing in all things, even in the least, to do the will of God from the heart and having every thought brought into captivity to the mind of the Spirit of God. Bless thy people; bless them in this way by saturating them with the Word of Thy truth.

C. H. Spurgeon, *C. H. Spurgeon's Prayers*, p. 125
[2 Corinthians 10:4–5; Colossians 3:16; Ephesians 6:17]

Lord, end my winter, and let my spring begin. I cannot with all my longing raise my soul out of her death and dulness, but all things are possible with Thee. I need celestial influences, the clear shinings of Thy love, the beams of Thy grace, the light of Thy countenance, these are the Pleiades to me. I suffer much from sin and temptation, these are my wintry signs, my terrible Orion. Lord, work wonders in me, and for me.

C. H. Spurgeon, *Morning and Evening*, p. 163 [Job 38:31]

Let your prayers climb the starry ladder, and get up to Christ Himself, and then, as you draw nigh to the blood-besprinkled mercy-seat, offer this prayer continually, "Lord, extend the kingdom of Thy dear Son." Such a petition, fervently presented, will elevate the spirit of all your devotions. Mind that you prove the sincerity of your prayer by labouring to promote the Lord's glory.

C. H. Spurgeon, *Morning and Evening*, p. 187 [Matthew 6:10]

Precious Lord Jesus, let me in very deed know the blessedness which dwells in abiding, unbroken fellowship with Thee. I am a poor worthless one, whose cheek Thou hast deigned to kiss! O let me kiss Thee in return with the kisses of my lips.

C. H. Spurgeon, *Morning and Evening*, p. 244 [Song of Solomon 1:2; 5:13]

We have had dark nights, but the star of love has shone forth amid the blackness. . . . We have gone through many trials, but never to our detriment, always to our advantage. . . . He who has been with us in six troubles, will not forsake us in the seventh. What we have known of our faithful God, proves that He will keep us to the end. . . . How can we ever be so ungenerous as to doubt our God? Lord, throw down the Jezebel of our unbelief, and let the dogs devour it.

C. H. Spurgeon, *Morning and Evening*, p. 582 [1 Samuel 27:1]

Great Shepherd, add to Thy mercies this one other, a heart to love Thee more truly as I ought.

C. H. Spurgeon, *Morning and Evening*, p. 583 [Isaiah 40:11]

It is easy to sing when we can read the notes by daylight; but he is skilful who sings when there is not a ray of light to read by—who sings from his heart. . . . It is not in man's power to sing when all is adverse, unless an altar-coal shall touch his lip. . . . O Thou chief musician, let us not remain songless because affliction is upon us, but tune Thou our lips to the melody of thanksgiving.

> C. H. Spurgeon, *Morning and Evening*, p. 587 [Job 35:10]

[Lord, grant us grace] . . . to mark the glow of the Spirit's light on the head of some saint who has risen up in spiritual stature, like Saul, above his fellows, till, like a mighty Alp, snowcapped, he reflects . . . the beams of the Sun of Righteousness, and bears the sheen of His effulgence high aloft for all to see, and seeing it, glorify His Father which is in heaven.

> C. H. Spurgeon, *Morning and Evening*, p. 588 [Ephesians 4:15; 2 Corinthians 3:18; 4:6; Matthew 5:16]

O God, look on the face of Thine anointed. Hear me by His name Who was full of tender compassion and wept over Jerusalem; by His love Who would not let the sinner die; by His heart which even after His death poured out a stream of blood and water for the sins of men. Lord, hear me, and save my brother; save my husband; save my child.

> C. H. Spurgeon, *Able to the Uttermost*, p. 180 [Psalm 84:9]

O Lord, we would dwell in Thy secret place, that abiding under Thy shadow we may live unharmed even where Satan's seat is, should Thy providence there pitch our tent.

> C. H. Spurgeon, *Flowers From a Puritan's Garden*, p. 145 [Psalm 91:1, 4]

O Lord, grant me grace to live above this world; and wherein I must live upon it, and think about it, help me to have few desires and no cares. Tune my nature so that without fail my life may make music to Thy praise.

> C. H. Spurgeon, *Flowers From a Puritan's Garden*, p. 141 [1 John 2:15–17]

O my most tender God and Father, I can never fully estimate the stoop of Thy majesty in deigning to love me, nor the greatness of Thy generosity in inviting me to have fellowship with Thee. Give me I pray Thee, grace to value such priceless goodness, and every day to live in habitual fellowship with Thee.

> C. H. Spurgeon, *Flowers From a Puritan's Garden*, p. 122
> [1 John 1:1–4]

Lord Jesus, be more real to our apprehensions, and so be more completely the Master of our affections.

> C. H. Spurgeon, *Flowers From a Puritan's Garden*, p. 125
> [John 14:21]

Sweet Lord Jesus, do Thou so anoint me that I may always bear about with me the fragrance of Thine infinite perfections, and be a savor of life unto life among my neighbors.

> C. H. Spurgeon, *Flowers From a Puritan's Garden*, p. 179
> [2 Corinthians 2:14–16]

Lord, make me hear Thy footfall evermore, and cause me to live as though I heard Thee at the door.

> C. H. Spurgeon, *Flowers From a Puritan's Garden*, p. 131
> [Revelation 3:20]

Lord, make me watchful in little matters, lest I grow careless in weightier concerns. Thou didst speak concerning the pins and cords of the tabernacle, and ordain that all should be made to pattern, and by this I perceive that Thou regardest even the small things of Thy service; I pray Thee, therefore, give me both clear light, a keen eye, and a tender heart, that in all things I may please Thee.

> C. H. Spurgeon, *Flowers From a Puritan's Garden*, p. 181
> [Exodus 38:20, 31]

O for living, loving, lasting union with the living Head!

> C. H. Spurgeon, *Flowers From a Puritan's Garden*, p. 186
> [John 17:21, 23, 26]

Our Lord can pour His grace into us altogether apart from means. . . . We are shallow and narrow creeks, and how can the great sea of divine love pour its fulness into us? O Lord, enlarge our hearts till we shall be "filled with all the fulness of God."

> C. H. Spurgeon, *Flowers From a Puritan's Garden*, p. 190
> [Ephesians 3:14–21]

Ah, Lord! Let me never sigh for ease, but always seek for usefulness. Square me till I am fit for a place in Thy temple; prune me till I yield my utmost fruit. I know not what this prayer may involve; but if I did, I would pray to be helped to pray it, and I would entreat Thee to fulfill it to the letter.

> C.H. Spurgeon, *Flowers From a Puritan's Garden*, p. 195 [John 15:1–7]

O my Lord, teach me to give Thee the choicest product of my being, and instruct me how to do this in the most acceptable manner. . . . If I am honoured to preach Thy gospel, may I plead for Thee with my whole heart, and speak even to a few as zealously as if thousands waited for my words.

> C. H. Spurgeon, *Flowers From a Puritan's Garden*, p. 205
> [Philippians 3:13–14]

Help us, O Purifier of the temple, to drive out all intruders, and reserve our soul in all the beauty of holiness for the Blessed and Only Potentate.

> C. H. Spurgeon, *Flowers From a Puritan's Garden*, p. 210
> [John 2:15]

O Thou destroyer of the serpent and his seed, break the head of sin within me, so that it may never lift up its usurped power within my soul. Let the sword of the Spirit do a thorough work within my nature, till not a single rebel lust shall remain alive in the wide domain of my being. Furbish Thy sword, O Captain of the Host, and do Thine office within me, for I cannot rest till sin is slain.

> C. H. Spurgeon, *Flowers From a Puritan's Garden*, p. 217
> [Romans 6:11; 7:24–25; 6:6]

Preachers and Preaching

With Spurgeon's *preaching* as your guide, your movements are not limited to some formal exercise on a barren asphalt area. . . . Hear him on such texts as "Accepted in the Beloved," "The Glory of His Grace." . . . Hear him on themes like these, and you have a sense of the vastness kindred to that which awes you when you listen to the Apostle Paul. Every apparently simple division in the sermon is like the turning of the telescope to some new galaxy of luminous wonders in the unfathomable sky.

> Jowett, *The Preacher: His Life and Work* (The Yale Lectures, 1911), pp. 93–94

Pastor G. H. Davies, of Lisbon, North Dakota, thus records Sheridan Knowles' remarkable prophecy: ". . . His name is Charles Spurgeon. He is only a boy, but he is the most wonderful *preacher* in the world. He is absolutely perfect in his oratory; and, besides that, a master in the art of acting. . . . His power was never equalled. Now, mark my word, boys, that young man will live to be the greatest preacher of this or any other age. He will bring more souls to Christ than any man who ever proclaimed the gospel, not excepting the apostle Paul. His name will be known everywhere, and his sermons will be translated into many of the languages of the world."

> C. H. Spurgeon Autobiography, Vol. 1, *The Early Years*, pp. 260–261

It is sadly common among ministers to add a word or subtract a word from the passage, or in some way to debase the language of sacred writ. Believers in verbal inspiration should be studiously careful to be verbally correct. Let us *quote the words as they stand* in the best possible translation, and it will be better still if we know the original, and can tell if our version fails to give the sense. How much mischief may arise out of an accidental alteration of the Word!

The Greatest Fight in the World, C. H. Spurgeon's "Final Manifesto," p. 23

We should resolve that we will *quote more of Holy Scripture.* Sermons should be full of Bible; sweetened, strengthened, sanctified with Bible essence. Bible hearers, when they hear indeed, come to be Bible lovers.

The Greatest Fight in the World, C. H. Spurgeon's "Final Manifesto," p. 24

True *preaching* is Artesian: it wells up from the great depth of the soul. If Christ has not made a well within us, there will be no outflow from us.

C. H. Spurgeon, *Metropolitan Tabernacle Pulpit,* Vol. 35, p. 615

An idler has no right in the pulpit. He is an instrument of Satan in damning the souls of men. The ministry demands brain labor. The *preacher* must read and study to keep his mind in good trim. Above all, he must put heart work into his preaching. He must feel what he *preaches.* It must never be with him an easy thing to deliver a sermon. He must feel as if he could *preach* his very life away before the sermon is done.

C. H. Spurgeon, *Metropolitan Tabernacle Pulpit,* Vol. 19, p. 462

You cannot leave out that part of the truth which is so dark and so solemn without weakening the force of all the other truths you *preach.* You rob of their brightness, and their urgent importance, the truths which concern salvation from the wrath to come. Brethren, leave out nothing. Be bold enough to *preach* unpalatable and unpopular truth.

> *The Greatest Fight in the World,* C. H. Spurgeon's "Final
> Manifesto," p. 35

Spurgeon fixed upon a text, and then, for many years, gave it to his secretary, who was a minister, in his great library, which he had indexed for him, and brought everything that had any bearing on that text, and piled books all around him. He took those books and read all those things, and then made his outline. That was his method.

> G. Campbell Morgan, *Preaching,* p. 46

What marvel if, under some men's shifty talk, people grow into love of both truth and falsehood! The fact is, they would like anything if only a clever deceiver would put it plausibly before them. They admire Moses and Aaron, but they would not say a word against Jannes and Jambres. We shall not join in the confederacy which seems to aim at such a comprehension. We must *preach* the gospel so distinctly that our people know what we are *preaching.* "If the trumpet give an uncertain sound, who shall prepare himself for the battle?" We shall not hesitate to speak in the strongest Saxon words we can find, and in the plainest sentences we can put together, that which we hold as *fundamental truth.*

> *The Greatest Fight in the World,* C. H. Spurgeon's "Final
> Manifesto," pp. 38–39

We must throw all our strength of judgment, memory, imagination, and eloquence into the delivery of the gospel; and not give to the *preaching* of the cross our random thoughts while wayside topics engross our deeper meditations.

> C. H. Spurgeon, *Lectures to My Students,* pp. 75–76

The *heart of preaching*, the throwing of the soul into it, the earnestness which pleads as for life itself, is half the battle as to gaining attention. . . . Have something to say, and say it earnestly, and the congregation will be at your feet.

C. H. Spurgeon, *Lectures to My Students*, p. 136

Especially is it the Holy Spirit's work to maintain in us a devotional frame of mind whilst we are discoursing. This is a condition to be greatly coveted—to continue praying while you are occupied with *preaching* . . . to keep the eye on the throne, and the wing in perpetual motion. . . . Oh, to burn in our secret heart while we blaze before the eyes of others! This is the work of the Spirit of God. Work it in us, O adorable Comforter!

C. H. Spurgeon, *Lectures to My Students*, p. 193

Mercury is usually lost in the rays of the sun; and that is where you and I ought to be, so close to Christ, the Sun of Righteousness, in our life and in our *preaching*, that the people who are trying to observe our movements can scarcely see us at all.

C. H. Spurgeon, *Lectures to My Students*, p. 426

Hear how Whitefield *preached*, and never dare to be lethargic again. Winter says of him that "sometimes he exceedingly wept, and was frequently so overcome, that for a few seconds you would suspect he never would recover; and when he did, nature required some little time to compose herself. I hardly ever knew him go through a sermon without weeping more or less. His voice was often interrupted by his affections; and I have heard him say in the pulpit, 'You blame me for weeping; but how can I help it, when you will not weep for yourselves, although your immortal souls are on the verge of destruction, and, for aught I know, you are

125

hearing your last sermon, and may never more have an opportunity to have Christ offered to you?'"

C. H. Spurgeon, *Lectures to My Students,* p. 307

If there be living water in your *preaching,* it may be very deep, but the light of truth will give clearness to it.

C. H. Spurgeon, *Lectures to My Students,* p. 210

Promises

The *promise* is the bow by which we shoot the arrows of supplication.

C. H. Spurgeon, *According to Promise,* p. 59

The *promises* exceed all measurement: there is an abyss of depth in them as to meaning, a heaven of height in them as to excellence, and an ocean of breadth in them as to duration.

C. H. Spurgeon, *According to Promise,* p. 62

Promises exhibit the fulness and all-sufficiency of God.

C. H. Spurgeon, *According to Promise,* p. 62

He who dives deepest by experience into the depths of the divine *promises* is fully aware that there is yet a lower depth of grace and love unfathomable.

C. H. Spurgeon, *According to Promise,* p. 63

The *promise* is longer than life, broader than sin, deeper than the grave, and higher than the clouds.

C. H. Spurgeon, *According to Promise,* p. 63

The more we believe the *promise,* the more we find in it to believe.

C. H. Spurgeon, *According to Promise,* p. 67

All depressing circumstances lose their power for evil when our faith takes firm hold upon the *promises* of God.

C. H. Spurgeon, *According to Promise*, p. 67

The divine *promise* should be as much written upon our hearts as upon the pages of the Book.

C. H. Spurgeon, *According to Promise*, p. 68

You will handle faith well if you are able to quote the *promises* of God against the attacks of your enemy.

C. H. Spurgeon, *The Treasury of the Bible*, Vol. 7, p. 451
[Ephesians 6:16]

Faith without a *promise* would be a foot without ground to stand upon.

C. H. Spurgeon, *According to Promise*, p. 51 [Hebrews 11:8–19]

The great father of the faithful saw the day of Christ through the telescope of God's *promise*, by the eye of faith.

C. H. Spurgeon, *According to Promise*, p. 52 [Hebrews 11:8–19]

We are persuaded to try the trembling legs of our faith by the sight of a *promise*.

C. H. Spurgeon, *According to Promise*, p. 58 [Hebrews 11:8–19]

Prayer takes the *promise* to the bank of faith, and obtains the golden blessing.

C. H. Spurgeon, *According to Promise*, p. 69 [2 Peter 1:4]

Many and many a time we have seen the dawn of heaven while we have beheld light breaking from the *promise*.

C. H. Spurgeon, *According to Promise*, p. 53 [Hebrews 11:24–29]

Faith has to bring all the faculties of the child of God upon their knees, and say to them, "Be quiet; listen while

God speaks." . . . "Wait, I say, on the Lord." May that which is written with ink in the Bible be written with grace on our hearts. May the public *promise* become a private *promise* to each one of us by the living experience of our own soul.

> C. H. Spurgeon, *The Treasury of the Bible*, Vol. 3, p. 85 [Psalm 119:162]

Have we clung to the naked *promise* of God and rested upon the bare arm of omnipotence, which in and of itself is more than sufficient for the fulfillment of every *promise?* O Lord, where are we? Where are we? Where shall we find an oasis of faith amid this wilderness of doubt? Where shall we find an Abraham?

> C. H. Spurgeon, *The Treasury of the Bible*, Vol. 6, p. 71 [Luke 18:8]

Our Master's field is very rich; behold the handfuls. See, there they lie before thee, poor timid believer! Gather them up, make them thine own, for Jesus bids thee take them. Be not afraid, only believe! Grasp these sweet *promises,* thresh them out by meditation and feed on them with joy.

> C. H. Spurgeon, *Morning and Evening*, p. 428 [Ruth 2:2]

Quote

You will handle faith well if you are able to *quote* the promises of God against the attacks of your enemy.

> C. H. Spurgeon, *The Treasury of the Bible*, Vol. 7, p. 451 [Ephesians 6:16]

Reflecting Christ

We must feed the flock of God. We must deal with eternal verities and grapple with heart and conscience. We must, in fact, live to educate a race of saints, in whom *the Lord Jesus* shall be *reflected* as in a thousand mirrors.

> C. H. Spurgeon, *Spurgeon's Sermons Preached on Unusual Occasions*, p. 181 [2 Corinthians 3:18 NIV]

Riches of Christ

My Master has *riches* beyond the count of arithmetic, the measurement of reason, the dream of imagination, or the eloquence of words. They are *unsearchable!*

> C. H. Spurgeon, *Morning and Evening*, p. 471 [Ephesians 3:8]

Salvation

If any man would be saved, he must believe that Jesus Christ is both *Lord* and *God.* Again, you must confess that Jesus Christ is *Lord,* that is, *Ruler* and *Master.* You must cheerfully become His disciple, follower, and servant. You must confess, "He is my *Master,* He is my *Lord.* I intend to be a soldier under Him. He shall be to me *Leader* and *Commander;* God has made Him such, and I accept Him as such." You are vocally to own Jesus; you are definitely and distinctly to say with your tongue, your mouth, your lips, that He is your *Lord* and *Saviour . . . .* With my mouth I do again confess the Lord Jesus, for I believe Him to be *very God of very God,* my *Master,* my *All.*

> C. H. Spurgeon, *Metropolitan Tabernacle Pulpit,* Vol. 32, pp. 247–248, 252 [Romans 10:9]

Faith is an act of the understanding; but it also proceeds from the heart. God gives *salvation* to faith because it resides next door to the affections, and is near akin to love; and love is the parent and the nurse of every holy feeling and act. Love to God is obedience, love to God is holiness.

129

To love God and to love man is to be conformed to the image of Christ; and this is *salvation*.

C. H. Spurgeon, *All of Grace*, p. 62 [Romans 10:9; John 14:21]

No sooner is the soul *quickened* than it at once discovers its lost estate, is horrified thereat, looks out for a refuge, and believing Christ to be a suitable one, *flies to Him and reposes in Him.*

C. H. Spurgeon, *Words of Warning for Daily Life*, pp. 69–70

To come to Jesus not only implies leaving all other confidences, and *trusting Christ*, it also means *following Him*. If you trust Him, you must obey Him. If you leave your soul in His hands, you must take Him to be *your Master*, and *your Lord*, as well as *your Saviour*. Christ has come to save you *from* sin, not *in* sin. He will make you holy.

C. H. Spurgeon, *Metropolitan Tabernacle Pulpit*, Sermon No. 2,349, p. 87 [John 6:37; 1 Peter 1:16]

Come just as you are, all guilty, empty, meritless, and fall before the great King, whom you have so often provoked, and beseech Him of His infinite mercy to blot out your transgressions, to change your nature, and to make you His own, and see if He will cast you away. Is it not written, "There is forgiveness with Thee, that Thou mayest be feared"? And again, "Him that cometh to me I will in no wise cast out."

C. H. Spurgeon, *Metropolitan Tabernacle Pulpit*, Vol. 26, p. 118 [John 6:37]

Submit yourselves. Yield to the grasp of those hands which were *nailed to the cross for you.*

C. H. Spurgeon, *Metropolitan Tabernacle Pulpit*, Sermon No. 1,910, p. 396 [John 6:37]

You must take Jesus to be your sole confidence, and then you must be obedient to His command, and take Him to be your *Master*, and *Lord.* Will you do that? If not, I have nothing to say to you except this,—he that believeth not in Him will perish without hope.

> C. H. Spurgeon, *Metropolitan Tabernacle Pulpit*, Sermon No.
> 2,349, p. 87 [John 6:37]

Jesus must be received as *King* as well as *Priest;* and where there is any hesitancy about this, the foundation of godliness is not yet laid.

> *The Best of C. H. Spurgeon*, p. 114

We are perilously likely to rest satisfied with a slight healing, and by this means to miss the great and complete *salvation* which comes from God alone. I wish to speak in deep earnestness to everyone here present upon this subject, for I have felt the power of it on my own soul. To deliver this message, I have made a desperate effort, quitting my sick-bed without due permit, moved by a restless pining to warn you against the counterfeits of the day.

> C. H. Spurgeon, *The Treasury of the Bible*, Vol. 4, pp. 34–35
> [Jeremiah 8:11; 17:14]

I am now speaking straight to every one of you, and I am setting myself in the middle pew that my keenest sentence may enter my own bosom as well as yours. I say, we are all of us in danger of being the subjects of a false healing: ministers, deacons, elders, church-members, aged professors, and young beginners—all alike. . . . The devil, who knows the exact bait for poor human nature, finds it easy to pacify an anxious mind by presenting a false *salvation,* and persuading the heart that all is well, while in fact nothing is well.

> C. H. Spurgeon, *The Treasury of the Bible*, Vol. 4, p. 35
> [Jeremiah 8:11; 17:14]

Unless you fix your eye upon the cross, and can answer, "I have believed in Jesus for *salvation,* and I still believe in Him. I have forsaken every evil way, and I am still striving against sin. I am a renewed man; I am struggling to the light, and struggling up to purity and to my God,"—unless, I say, you can give such firm and solid answers, there will be hard times for you, and deep depressions far more grievous than the physical pain could possibly bring to you. I pray you therefore do not put off making sure work for eternity. . . . O brethren, if there be any error about your profession get it right *now.* . . . True healing must be radical. Oh pray to have it so! The healing which we need must go to the root of the business, and work a thorough change.

> C. H. Spurgeon, *The Treasury of the Bible,* Vol. 4, p. 36
> [Jeremiah 8:11; 17:14]

The law is a storm which wrecks your hopes of *self-salvation,* but washes you upon the Rock of Ages.

> *Charles Spurgeon: The Best From All His Works,* p. 21

Though nowadays we hear of persons being healed before they have been wounded and brought into a certainty of justification without ever having lamented their condemnation, we are very dubious as to the value of such healings and justifyings. This style of things is not according to the truth. God never clothes men until He has first stripped them, nor does He quicken them by the gospel till first they are slain by the law. When you meet with persons in whom there is no trace of conviction of sin, you may be quite sure that they have not been wrought upon by the Holy Spirit, for "when He is come, He will reprove the world of sin, and of righteousness, and of judgment." Great care must be taken that faith is exercised upon Christ for a complete *salvation* and not for a part of it.

> *The Best of C. H. Spurgeon,* p. 111

Sanctification

Still the gospel breaks, and still it makes whole; still it wounds, and still it quickens; still it seems to hurl men down to hell in their terrible experience of the evil of sin, but still it lifts them up into an ecstatic joy, till they are exalted almost to heaven when they lay hold upon it, and feel its power in their souls. The gospel that was a gospel of births and deaths, of killing and making alive, in the days of John Bunyan, has just the same effect upon our hearts today, when it comes with the power that God has put into it by His Spirit. It produces the same results, and the same *sanctifying* influence as it ever had.

> C. H. Spurgeon, *Metropolitan Tabernacle Pulpit*, Sermon No. 2,358, p. 198 [Hebrews 13:8]

Saturated in Scripture

I would rather lay my soul asoak in half a dozen verses all day than I would, as it were, rinse my hand in several chapters. Oh, to bathe in a *text of Scripture* till it *saturates your heart!* . . . Set your heart upon God's Word! It is the only way to know it thoroughly: let your whole nature be *plunged into it* as cloth into a dye.

> C. H. Spurgeon, *Metropolitan Tabernacle Pulpit*, Vol. 27, p. 42 [Colossians 3:16; Ephesians 6:17]

In proportion as your mind becomes *saturated with Holy Scripture*, you are conscious of being lifted right up, and carried aloft as on eagles' wings.

> *The Greatest Fight in the World*, C. H. Spurgeon's "Final Manifesto," p. 19

Better six words of one verse bedewed with the Holy Spirit than to routinely read one hundred chapters of the Bible.

> C. H. Spurgeon (paraphrased)

Oh, that we might know the *Spirit of Holy Scripture* thoroughly, drinking it in, till we are *saturated with it!* This is the blessing which we resolve to obtain.

The Greatest Fight in the World, C. H. Spurgeon's "Final
Manifesto," p. 23

There are certain people who think if they read a good long bit of Bible, they've done a great deal. . . . The mere outward fashion and form of Bible reading will not profit anybody. One bit of Bible prayed over, and bedewed with the *Spirit,* and made alive, though it be only a short sentence of six words, will profit you more than a hundred chapters without the *Spirit,* because the hundred chapters without the *Spirit* are flesh—dead; but the one verse with the *Spirit* is the thing that quickeneth.

The Best of C. H. Spurgeon, p. 218

The divine promise should be as much *written upon our hearts* as upon the pages of the Book.

C. H. Spurgeon, *According to Promise,* p. 68

Lord . . . May Thy Word be the supreme ruler of our being. May we give ourselves up to its sacred law to be obedient to its every hint, wishing in all things, even in the least, to do the will of God from the heart and having every thought brought into captivity to the mind of the Spirit of God. Bless Thy people; bless them in this way by *saturating* them with the Word of Thy truth.

C. H. Spurgeon, *C. H. Spurgeon's Prayers,* p. 125
[2 Corinthians 10:4–5; Colossians 3:16; Ephesians 6:17]

Scripture

Christ chose this weapon *[the Word]* out of all the others, and used it in His earliest conflict, so, too, *He used it when no man was near.* The value of *Holy Scripture* is not alone seen in public teaching or striving for the truth, its still small voice is equally powerful when the servant of the Lord is enduring personal trial in the lone wilderness. The severest struggles of a true Christian are usually unknown to any but himself. Not in the family do we meet the most subtle temptations, but in the closet, not in the shop so much as in the recesses of our own spirit do we wrestle with principalities and powers. For these dread duels, *"It is written"* is the best sword and shield. *Scripture* to convince another man is good; but *Scripture* is most required to console, defend and sanctify our own soul.

> C. H. Spurgeon, *Spurgeon's Expository Encyclopedia*, Vol. 15, p. 222 [Matthew 4:4; Ephesians 6:17]

The Holy Ghost rides in the chariot of *Scripture,* and not in the wagon of modern thought.

> C. H. Spurgeon, *Metropolitan Tabernacle Pulpit*, Vol. 37, p. 233 [Ephesians 6:17]

Sermons

We should resolve that we will quote more of Holy Scripture. *Sermons* should be full of Bible; sweetened, strengthened, sanctified with Bible essence. Bible hearers, when they hear indeed, come to be Bible lovers.

> *The Greatest Fight in the World*, C.H. Spurgeon's "Final Manifesto," p. 24

The Holy Spirit will never set His seal to falsehood. Never! If what you preach is not the truth, God will not own it. If we do not *speak clear doctrine with plainness of speech,* the Holy Spirit will not put His signature to our empty prating.

> *The Greatest Fight in the World*, C. H. Spurgeon's "Final Manifesto," p. 61

Your *sermons*—make them red hot; never mind if men say you are too enthusiastic or even too fanatical.

> C. H. Spurgeon, *The Soul Winner*, p. 75

An idler has no right in the pulpit. He is an instrument of Satan in damning the souls of men. The ministry demands brain labor. The preacher must read and study to keep his mind in good trim. Above all, he must put heart work into his preaching. He must feel what he preaches. It must never be with him an easy thing to deliver a *sermon*. He must feel as if he could preach his very life away before the *sermon* is done.

> C. H. Spurgeon, *Metropolitan Tabernacle Pulpit*, Vol. 19,
> p. 462

Sin

The period of my conviction of *sin* is burned into my memory as with a red-hot iron. Its wounds are cured, but the scars remain. There I stood, *fearing* every moment lest I should be crushed into the abyss and justly lost forever.

> C. H. Spurgeon, *Metropolitan Tabernacle Pulpit*, Vol. 18,
> p. 485

"If ye do not go forth to the battles of the Lord, and contend for the Lord God and for His people, ye do *sin* against the Lord: and be sure your *sin* will find you out." The *sin* of doing nothing is about the biggest of all *sins*, for it involves most of the others. . . . Horrible idleness! God save us from it!

> C. H. Spurgeon, *Words of Wisdom for Daily Life*, pp. 136–137
> [Numbers 32:20–23]

The highest flights of human devotion must end in confession of *sin;* "I have gone astray."

> C. H. Spurgeon, *The Treasury of David*, Vol. 3, Pt. 1, p. 479
> [Psalm 119:176]

Sorrow

It is in our most desperate *sorrows* that we have our happiest experiences. You must go to Patmos to see the revelation. It is only on the barren, storm-girt rock, shut out from all the world's light, that we can find a fitting darkness in which we can view the light of heaven undistracted by the shadows of earth.

C. H. Spurgeon, *Gleanings Among the Sheaves*, pp. 11–12

Study

Earnestness . . . is diminished by neglect of *study*.

C. H. Spurgeon, *Lectures to My Students*, p. 310

Submission

Believing is the *submission* of the soul to God's truth, the yielding of the heart to God's salvation.

C. H. Spurgeon, *Able to the Uttermost*, p. 141 [Hebrews 4:3]

Submit yourselves. Yield to the grasp of those hands which were nailed to the cross for you.

C. H. Spurgeon, *Metropolitan Tabernacle Pulpit*, Sermon No. 1,910, p. 396 [John 6:37]

Substitution (God's Anointed)

"Look upon the face of *Thine anointed*."—(Psalm 84:9) . . . God alone knows all He sees in Christ, but when He sees Him, He is full of love to us because of what He sees in Him. It is well for us to recollect that our salvation does not rest upon our seeing Christ so much as it does upon God's seeing Him. We are not saved except we see Him, truly, but then the real foundation of our salvation lies in God seeing Christ.

C. H. Spurgeon, *Able to the Uttermost*, p. 178 [Psalm 84:9]

Beloved friend, I put this prayer into your mouth; may God put it into your heart. Say, "O God, I am vile and sinful: look not on me, but look on *Thine anointed.* I shelter in His wounds. Be not angry with me, though I deserve it, but let Thy love to Him constrain Thee to show Thy love to me!"

C. H. Spurgeon, Able to the Uttermost, p. 178 [Psalm 84:9]

Say, "Oh, for His sake, by His agony and bloody sweat, by His cross and passion, by His precious death and burial, by His glorious resurrection and ascension, have mercy on me, O God!" . . . Might not any backsliding child of God use just the same prayer tonight? . . . And might not this suit any Christian here who has been hard at work for Christ? You know, brethren, I believe those who work hardest for Christ are those who are most conscious that their work is not fit to be accepted in itself.

C. H. Spurgeon, Able to the Uttermost, p. 179 [Psalm 84:9]

Have you tried this argument, "O God, look on the face of *Thine anointed.* Hear me by His name Who was full of tender compassion and wept over Jerusalem; by His love Who would not let the sinner die; by His heart which even after His death poured out a stream of blood and water for the sins of men. Lord, hear me, and save my brother, save my husband; save my child." Would not that be good pleading?

C. H. Spurgeon, Able to the Uttermost, p. 180 [Psalm 84:9]

Beloved friends, we very calmly and coolly talk about this thing, but it is the greatest marvel in the universe; it is the miracle of earth, the mystery of heaven, the terror of hell. Could we fully realize the guilt of sin, the punishment due to it, and the literal *substitution of Christ,* it would work in us an intense enthusiasm of gratitude, love, and praise.

> C. H. Spurgeon, *Till He Come,* p. 338 [John 1:29; 1 Peter 2:24–25; Psalm 84:9]

We would have the Lord look upon our Bridegroom's face. We have no comeliness, but He gives us all His beauty. When He took us, He took us as we were, but He made us to be as He is. He took our foulness, but He gave us all His righteousness; and we therefore say, "Lord, when Thou lookest on the family, do not come and look at the spouse. Come not and look at the weaker vessel, but if Thou regardest the house look at the house-band, the husband, the head, the Lord, the Master. He is our strength; He is our representative."

> C. H. Spurgeon, *Able to the Uttermost,* pp. 175–176 [Psalm 84:9]

I scarcely know a prayer that would better become our lips when they are praying their last prayer on earth, and getting ready for their first song in Heaven, than to say here, "Behold, O God our shield, and look upon the face of *Thine anointed,*" and then the moment the prayer was over to have to say, "My God, I also have looked upon the face of *Thine anointed,* and now that the beatific vision has charmed me into bliss I have forgotten all the pains of dying; I have reached immortality and life; for I see the anointed of the Lord Who is for ever now my shield from death."

> C. H. Spurgeon, *Able to the Uttermost,* p. 180 [Psalm 84:9]

Supplication

Supplication, in which a man's proper self is not thoroughly present in agonizing earnestness and vehement desire, is utterly ineffectual.

> C. H. Spurgeon, *Morning and Evening,* p. 31 [Psalm 109:4; James 5:16]

Desires and longings are the essence of *supplication,* and it little matters what shape they take. "O that" is as acceptable a prayer as "Our Father."

> C. H. Spurgeon, *The Treasury of David,* Vol. 3, Pt. 1, p. 144
> [Psalm 119:5]

The promise is the bow by which we shoot the arrow of *supplication.*

> C. H. Spurgeon, *According to Promise,* p. 59

Earnestness is the life of *supplication.*

> C. H. Spurgeon

Tears

To continue still to mourn sin is to continue to grow in grace. *Tear drops* are blessed watering for the flowers of grace.

> C. H. Spurgeon, *Able to the Uttermost,* p. 30 [Luke 23:27–28]

The way from the higher state to the very highest is very much a road that is watered by *tears.*

> C. H. Spurgeon, *Able to the Uttermost,* p. 30 [Luke 23:27–28]

You . . . never see the atonement so well as through your *tears.* Believe me, John Bunyan was right when he put Mr. Wet-eyes to go with the petition from the town of Mansoul to Prince Emmanuel; and I believe that Mr. Wet-eyes is clearer-sighted than most, and when the *teardrop* is in the eye it acts like a telescopic glass.

> Oh, let me *weep* for naught but sin,
>   And after none but Thee!
> And then I would (oh, that I might!)
>   A constant *weeper* be.
>
> > C. H. Spurgeon, *Able to the Uttermost,* p. 151 [Leviticus
> > 23:27–40]

Temptation

Christ chose this weapon [the Word] out of all the others, and used it in his earliest conflict, so, too, He used it when no man was near. The value of Holy Scripture is not alone seen in public teaching or striving for the truth; its still small voice is equally powerful when the servant of the Lord is enduring *personal trial* in the lone wilderness. The *severest struggles* of a true Christian are usually unknown to any but himself. Not in the family do we meet the most *subtle temptations*, but in the closet, not in the shop so much as in the recesses of our own spirit do we *wrestle with principalities and powers.* For these *dread duels*, "It is written" is the best sword and shield. Scripture to convince another man is good; but Scripture is most required to console, defend and sanctify our own soul.

> C. H. Spurgeon, *Spurgeon's Expository Encyclopedia*, Vol. 15,
> p. 222 [Matthew 4:4; Ephesians 6:17]

Think

It is a grand thing to be driven to *think*, it is a grander thing to be driven to pray through having been made to *think*.

> C. H. Spurgeon, *Spurgeon's Expository Encyclopedia*, Vol. 15,
> p. 211 [Matthew 12:3–7]

Transformed

A sight of Jesus by faith is the pleasure of beholding Him in His glory and being *transformed* into His image.

> C. H. Spurgeon, *Faith's Checkbook*, p. 67 [2 Corinthians 3:18]

Faith sees God with a *transforming* look. . . . The glory of God in the face of Jesus Christ yields us Heaven below, and it will be to us the Heaven of Heaven above.

> C. H. Spurgeon, *Faith's Checkbook*, p. 139 [2 Corinthians 4:6]

Trial(s)

It is said that when the stars cannot be seen during the day from the ordinary level of the earth, if one should go down into a dark well, they would be visible at once. And certainly it is a fact that the best of God's promises are usually seen by His Church when she is in her darkest *trials*.

> C. H. Spurgeon, *Gleanings Among the Sheaves*, p. 11

Great faith must have great *trials*. Mr. Great-heart would never have been Mr. Great-heart if he had not once been Mr. Great-trouble.

> C. H. Spurgeon, *Gleanings Among the Sheaves*, p. 40

One of the sweet necessities of *trial* is to bring forth and use those precious graces which else had been unemployed.

> C. H. Spurgeon (probably quoting Thomas Manton), *Flowers From a Puritan's Garden*, p. 78

Spices are most fragrant when burnt and bruised, so have saving graces their chiefest fragrancy in *hard times*. The pillar that conducted the Israelites appeared as a cloud by day, but as a fire by night. The excellency of faith is beclouded till it be put upon a thorough *trial*.

> C. H. Spurgeon (probably quoting Thomas Manton), *Flowers From a Puritan's Garden*, p. 78

Trinity

The glory of the divine *Trinity* overawes us until we behold the milder radiance of the Incarnate God.

> C. H. Spurgeon, *According to Promise*, p. 125 [2 Corinthians 1:20]

O God, we praise Thee for keeping us. . . . Blessed be the Lord for every office sustained by *each divine person*, and for the divine blessing which has come streaming down to us through each one of those condescending titles worn by the *Father, Son, and the Holy Spirit.*

> C. H. Spurgeon, *C. H. Spurgeon's Prayers*, p. 14 [Jude 24–25; 2 Corinthians 13:14]

In proportion as we have more regard for the sacred *Godhead,* the wondrous *Trinity* in Unity, shall we see a greater display of God's power and a more glorious manifestation of His might in our churches.

> C. H. Spurgeon, *Metropolitan Tabernacle Pulpit*, Vol. 1, p. 379

Keep the existence of the *Trinity* prominent in your ministry. . . . Salvation requires a *Trinity,* so does that very breath by which we live.

> C. H. Spurgeon, *Metropolitan Tabernacle Pulpit*, Vol. 37, p. 374 [John 16:14–15]

He is a *triune* God: render Him *triune* praise. Bless Him; bless Him; bless Him; be always blessing Him.

> C. H. Spurgeon, *Metropolitan Tabernacle Pulpit*, Vol. 36, p. 8 [Psalm 103:1]

A gospel without the *Trinity!* It is a rope of sand that cannot hold together.

> C. H. Spurgeon, *Metropolitan Tabernacle Pulpit*, Vol. 1, p. 29

Trouble

Wherever you find great fogs of *trouble,* and mists of sorrow, you always find emerald green hearts: full of the beautiful verdure of the comfort and love of God.

> C. H. Spurgeon, *Words of Cheer for Daily Life*, p. 25

Better an ocean of *trouble* than a drop of sin.

> C. H. Spurgeon, *Words of Cheer for Daily Life*, p. 129

All the *troubles* of a Christian do but wash him nearer Heaven; the rough winds do but hurry his passage across the straits of this life to the port of eternal peace.

C. H. Spurgeon, *Words of Cheer for Daily Life*, p. 130

Great hearts can only be made by great *troubles*. The spade of *trouble* digs the reservoir of comfort deeper, and makes more room for consolation.

C. H. Spurgeon, *Words of Cheer for Daily Life*, p. 24
[2 Corinthians 1:3–5]

A ploughman . . . said to me, "Depend upon it, if you or I ever get one inch above the ground, we shall get just that inch too high." I believe it is true; for the lower we lie, the nearer to the ground we are—the more our *troubles* humble us—the more fit we are to receive comfort; and God always gives us comfort when we are most fit for it.

C. H. Spurgeon, *Words of Cheer for Daily Life*, p. 24
[2 Corinthians 1:3–5]

Trust

Trust is one of the sublimest forms of adoration.

C. H. Spurgeon, *Metropolitan Tabernacle Pulpit*, Vol. 33,
p. 466 [Ephesians 1:12–13]

Truth

We can learn nothing of the gospel except by feeling its *truths*.

The Best of C. H. Spurgeon, p. 49 [John 14:21]

Sooner than deny the *truth*, we must forego every . . . honour, every particle of deserved esteem, every rag of repute. . . . In the battle for the *truth*, let your personal comfort and reputation go to the winds. . . . My Lord, for Thee I will rejoice to be "the offscouring of all things," that I may be found faithful to Thee and to Thy *truth,* even to the end.

C. H. Spurgeon, *An All-Round Ministry,* p. 307

We should guard ourselves against compromising the *truth* of God by association with those who do not hold it, especially at such a time as this.

C. H. Spurgeon, *An All-Round Ministry,* p. 311

Yield in all things personal, but be firm where *truth* and holiness are concerned.

C. H. Spurgeon, *An All-Round Ministry,* p. 277

Believe in the inspired volume up to the hilt. Believe it with the whole strength of your being. Let the *truths* of Scripture become the chief factors in your life, the chief operating forces of your action.

The Greatest Fight in the World, C. H. Spurgeon's "Final Manifesto," p. 24

The Holy Spirit will never set His seal to falsehood. Never! If what you preach is not the *truth,* God will not own it. If we do not speak clear doctrine with plainness of speech, the Holy Spirit will not put His signature to our empty prating.

The Greatest Fight in the World, C. H. Spurgeon's "Final Manifesto," p. 61

You cannot leave out that part of the *truth* which is so dark and so solemn without weakening the force of all the other *truths* you preach. You rob of their brightness, and their urgent importance, the *truths* which concern salvation from the wrath to come. Brethren, leave out nothing. Be bold enough to preach unpalatable and unpopular *truth.*

The Greatest Fight in the World, C. H. Spurgeon's "Final Manifesto," p. 35

What marvel if, under some men's shifty talk, people grow into love of both *truth* and falsehood! The fact is, they would like anything if only a clever deceiver would put it plausibly before them. They admire Moses and Aaron, but they would not say a word against Jannes and Jambres. We shall not join in the confederacy which seems to aim at such a comprehension. We must preach the gospel so distinctly that our people know what we are preaching. "If the trumpet give an uncertain sound, who shall prepare himself for the battle?" We shall not hesitate to speak in the strongest Saxon words we can find, and in the plainest sentences we can put together, that which we hold as *fundamental truth.*

The Greatest Fight in the World, C. H. Spurgeon's "Final Manifesto," pp. 38–39

We are very careful to use our best language when proclaiming *eternal truths* in this battle against false doctrine.

The Greatest Fight in the World, C. H. Spurgeon's "Final Manifesto," p. 6

My topics have to do with our life-work, with the crusade against error and sin in which we are engaged. I hope that every man here is pledged to do and dare for Christ and for His cross, and never to be satisfied till Christ's foes are routed and Christ Himself is satisfied. Our fathers used to speak of "The Cause of God and *Truth*"; and it is for this that we bear arms, the few against the many, the feeble against the mighty. Oh, to be found good soldiers of Jesus Christ!

The Greatest Fight in the World, C. H. Spurgeon's "Final Manifesto," pp. 8–9

To see the effects of the *truth* of God in the lives of holy men is confirmatory to faith and stimulating to holy aspiration.

The Greatest Fight in the World, C. H. Spurgeon's "Final Manifesto," p. 20

We want churches that know the *truth,* and are well taught in the things of God. If we taught better they would learn better. See how little many professors know; not enough to give them discernment between *living truth* and deadly error. Old-fashioned believers could give you chapter and verse for what they believed; but how few of such remain! To try to shake them was by no means a hopeful task: you might as well have hoped to shake the pillars of the universe; for they were steadfast, and could not be carried about with every wind of doctrine. They knew what they knew, and they held fast that which they had learned. Oh, for a church of out-and-out believers, impervious to the soul-destroying doubt which pours upon us in showers!

The Greatest Fight in the World, C. H. Spurgeon's "Final Manifesto," pp. 45–46 [Ephesians 4:14; Romans 6:17]

The Holy Spirit makes no promise to bless compromises. If we make a treaty with error or sin, we do it at our own risk. If we do anything that we are not clear about, if we tamper with *truth* or holiness, if we are friends of the world, if we make provision for the flesh, if we preach half-heartedly and are in league with errorists, we have no promise that the Holy Spirit will go with us. If you want to know what great things the Lord can do, as the Lord God Almighty, be separate from the world, and from those who apostatize from the *truth.* The man of God will have nothing to do with Sodom, or with false doctrine. If you see anything that is evil, give it the cut direct. Have done with those who have done with the *truth.*

The Greatest Fight in the World, C. H. Spurgeon's "Final Manifesto," pp. 59–60

I have been charged with being a mere echo of the Puritans, but I had rather be the echo of *truth,* than the voice of falsehood.

C. H. Spurgeon, *An All-Round Ministry,* p. 10

We declare that there are certain *verities,*—essential, abiding, eternal—from which it is ruinous to swerve.

C. H. Spurgeon, *An All-Round Ministry,* p. 9

The *truth* of God is the best of all guests; entertain it, as Abraham did the angels. Spare not the best you have for its maintenance; for it leaves a rich blessing with those who deny themselves for it.

C. H. Spurgeon, *An All-Round Ministry,* p. 341

Be *true,* and dare all things. . . . Lose all for the *truth* if need be.

C. H. Spurgeon, *An All-Round Ministry,* pp. 378–379

There will always be trouble in the churches so long as men are afraid to denounce sin and error. . . . I make no personal reference, but I see the spirit of compromise concerning holiness and sin, *truth* and error, far too prevalent. The spirit of compromise comes not of the Spirit of God, but of the spirit of the world. It is always wisest and best to exhibit clear decision upon *fundamental points;* we must draw the line distinctly, and then stand to it firmly. . . . If any shall brand us with epithets, such as "bigot," "vulgar dogmatist," or "mere echo of departed Puritanism," (and all these have been used), we will only reply, "You may apply to us what opprobrious titles you please, but we know that, if we were to express the *truth* about you, there is no adjective of contempt which you do not deserve; and, therefore, because we know of no language sufficiently strong to set forth our abhorrence of your *false doctrine*, we will let you pass in silence."

C. H. Spurgeon, *An All-Round Ministry*, pp. 291, 26

The right path runs through a solitary land, and if thou darest not travel alone, thou wilt never reach the Celestial City! . . . Continual consorting with those who have no sympathy with the *great truths* of the gospel, is running into perpetual peril. For my part, I find association with persons of loose views a thing too painful for me.

C. H. Spurgeon, *An All-Round Ministry*, p. 292

Go over the *fundamental truths* with your hearers very carefully. The bulk of the people do not know the *first principles* of the gospel. . . . Let us go over the *foundation truths* again and again. . . . Go over the *elementary truths* with your people. Make them know the *first principles* of the faith. . . . It will bless them, and many of them will be delighted. . . . Paul wrote to the Philippians, "To write the *same things* to you, to me indeed is not grievous, but for you it is safe."

C. H. Spurgeon, *An All-Round Ministry*, pp. 308–309
[Philippians 3:1]

They are trying in certain quarters, to make the *cardinal points of truth* go round with the wind.

C. H. Spurgeon, *An All-Round Ministry*, p. 287

Nails which are important to a structure must be driven in with diligence. Foundation stones should be lain with scrupulous care; and *truth*, which is *fundamental*, should be repeated by the teacher till the disciple has learned it beyond all fear of ever forgetting it.

C. H. Spurgeon

As for me, my heart is quiet beneath the contumely which comes of defending the *Lord's own truth*, for He will justify me before long; and if He should not do so speedily, yet He will do it ultimately: yea, I am happy to wait even till after death, for I know that my justifier liveth, and that, though after my skin worms devour this body, yet shall my Lord vindicate me and all others who have been faithful to *His truth.*

> C. H. Spurgeon, *Metropolitan Tabernacle Pulpit,* Vol. 35, p. 77
> [Micah 7:7]

The Lord has placed His treasure of *truth,* not in the golden vase of talent, but in the earthen vessels of lowly minds.

> C. H. Spurgeon, *Metropolitan Tabernacle Pulpit,* Vol. 35, p. 77
> [2 Corinthians 4:7; 1 Corinthians 2:12]

A good man's hate of falsehood is as intense as his love of *truth;* it must necessarily be so. . . . In these days there are many men to whom the *truths* of Scripture are like a pack of cards, to be shuffled as occasion suits. To them peace and quietness are jewels, and *truth* is as the mire of the streets. . . . To the man that is loyal to his Lord, and faithful to his convictions, it can never be so; he hates the teaching which belies his God. He that has never felt his blood boil against *error* which robs God of His glory does not love the law, nor will he know that great peace which comes by having the law enshrined in the heart.

> C. H. Spurgeon, *Metropolitan Tabernacle Pulpit,* Vol. 34, p. 41
> [Psalm 119:165]

We do not know the *truth* aright unless it makes us holy. We do not hold *truth* in a *true* way unless it leads us to a *true* life. If you use the back of a knife it will not cut: *truth* hath its handle and its blade; see that you use it properly. You can make pure water kill a man; you must use every good thing aright. . . . The *truth,* when fully used, will daily destroy sin, nourish grace, suggest noble desires, and urge to holy acts.

> C. H. Spurgeon, *Metropolitan Tabernacle Pulpit*, Vol. 32,
> pp. 155–156 [John 17:17]

Thoughtlessness is the prolific mother of iniquity. It is a hopeful sign when minds begin to roam among *lofty truths.* The man who has been taught of God to think will not so readily sin as the being whose mind is buried beneath his flesh.

> C. H. Spurgeon, *Metropolitan Tabernacle Pulpit*, Vol. 29,
> p. 455 [Romans 6:14–15; John 17:17]

Ye knights of *truth,* charge home! Spare not, but slay; let error die before you, until *truth,* and *truth* alone, shall sit king over the whole world!

> C. H. Spurgeon, *The New Park Street Pulpit*, Vol. 2, p. 116
> [Jude 3; Revelation 3:4]

True regeneration is never repeated, and it is the commencement of a life which will know no end, either in time or in eternity. Now anything which is to last must be expensive. You shall get your glass coloured, if you will cheaply, but the sun will soon remove all its beauty. If you would obtain a glass which shall retain its colour for centuries, every single step in the process of its manufacture will be costly, involving much labour and great care. So it is with *true* religion. You may get it cheap if you will, it will look quite as well as the real thing, and for a little while it will bring you almost all the . . . respect which the genuine article would have brought you; but it will not last.

> C. H. Spurgeon, *The Treasury of the Bible*, Vol. 5, p. 888 [Luke
> 14:28–30]

Spurgeon was "a voice crying in the wilderness." . . . His voice lives on to speak in written form, to other generations.

His sermons are perhaps his greatest living legacy, but his strict adherence to *Truth* . . . has lessons for us.

> The Publisher, *The Sword and the Trowel,* February 1892,
> p. 93 [John 14:6, 17:17; James 3:17]

If there be living water in your preaching, it may be very deep, but the light of *truth* will give clearness to it.

> C. H. Spurgeon, *Lectures to My Students,* p. 210

Unbelief

Ah, my brethren, when you think of *unbelief* as aiming her darts at Jesus Christ, the Well-beloved of our soul, surely you will say that it is a shameful sin, and a disgraceful crime against infinite love!

> C. H. Spurgeon, *Spurgeon's Expository Encyclopedia,* Vol. 15,
> p. 87 [Mark 16:14]

Unbelief degrades us into beasts whose carcasses fall beneath the poleaxe of judgment. Oh, that we might all be rid of *unbelief,* that degrading, desecrating, defiling, destroying thing!

> C. H. Spurgeon, *Spurgeon's Expository Encyclopedia,* Vol. 15,
> p. 82 [Hebrews 3:17]

Beloved, may God render this *unbelief* impossible by sending such life floods of grace through all the members of Christ's body that never more shall a single thought of *mistrust* of our glorious covenant Head enter our minds even for a single instant!

> C. H. Spurgeon, *Spurgeon's Expository Encyclopedia,* Vol. 15,
> p. 88 [Mark 16:14]

Unbelief withers every virtue in the bud.

> C. H. Spurgeon, *Gleanings Among the Sheaves,* p. 29

Unbelief is an evil thing in itself. . . . Think how you would feel if others *disbelieved* you.

> C. H. Spurgeon, *Spurgeon's Expository Encyclopedia*, Vol. 15, p. 86 [Mark 16:14]

Virtues without faith are whitewashed sins. *Unbelief* nullifies everything.

> C. H. Spurgeon, *Gleanings Among the Sheaves*, p. 29

How can we ever be so ungenerous as to doubt our God? Lord, throw down the Jezebel of our *unbelief*, and let the dogs devour it.

> C. H. Spurgeon, *Morning and Evening*, p. 582 [1 Samuel 27:1]

Unearnest Minister

Among all who will need eternal compassion, surely the unfaithful, unholy, *unearnest minister* of Christ will be the most pitiable! What did I say? Nay, rather the most contemptible, the most despicable, the most accursed! Surely, every thunderbolt shall make his brow its target, and every arrow of God shall seek his conscience as its mark. If I must perish, let me suffer anyhow but as a minister who has desecrated the pulpit by a slumbering style of ministry, by a want of passion for souls. How shall such men answer for it at the bar of God—the smooth things, the polite and honeyed words, the daubing of men with the untempered mortar of peace, peace, when they should have dealt with them honestly as in God's name? Oh, sirs, if we never play the Boanerges, we shall hear God's thunders in our ears, and that for ever and ever, and cursed of men, and cursed of the Most High, shall we be without end. In Tophet we shall have this wail peculiar to ourselves, "We preached what we did not feel; we testified of what we did not know; men received not our witness, for we were hypocrites and deceivers, and

153

now we go down, richly deserving it, to the very lowest depths of perdition."

> C. H. Spurgeon, *Words of Warning for Daily Life*, pp. 101–102 [Jude 4–13; Matthew 7:15–23]

Unseen and Eternal

Have you left the rut of present sensual perception for the way of faith in the *unseen and eternal?*

> C. H. Spurgeon, *According to Promise*, p. 19 [2 Corinthians 4:18]

Vine

The *vine* is of all trees the most useless unless it bears fruit. . . . It must either bear fruit, or else it must be consumed in the fire.

> C. H. Spurgeon, *We Endeavour*, p. 89 [John 15:6]

The *vine* is constantly used in Scripture as a picture of the nominal Church of Christ; so, like the *vine,* we must either bring forth fruit or we shall be accounted as good for nothing. We must serve God, we must bring forth, from our very soul, love to God and service to Him as the fruit of our renewed nature, or else we are useless, worthless, and shall only abide our time, and then we shall be cut down to be burned . . . "flung over the wall as a useless thing to be burned."

> C. H. Spurgeon

Weakness

All men who are eminently useful, are made to feel their *weakness* in a supreme degree.

> C. H. Spurgeon

Our *weakness* shall be our strength, for God shall make it to be the platform upon which the omnipotence of His grace shall be displayed.

C. H. Spurgeon, *Words of Counsel for Christian Workers*, p. 23

Wealth

The snow melts not sooner than the joy of *wealth,* and the smoke of the chimney is as solid as the comfort of riches!

C. H. Spurgeon, *Words of Wisdom for Daily Life*, p. 24
[1 Corinthians 7:29–31]

Will of God

Blessed is the man whose life is a practical transcript of the *will of God.*

Charles Spurgeon: The Best From All His Works, p. 232

Wise

The really *wise* . . . are too well instructed to be ignorant of their own ignorance.

C. H. Spurgeon, *Christ's Incarnation*, p. 98 [Matthew 2:2]

In the case of these *wise* men, we see *ignorance admitted.* Truly *wise* men are never above asking questions. . . . The knowledge of our ignorance is the doorstep of the temple of knowledge.

C. H. Spurgeon, *Christ's Incarnation*, p. 98 [Matthew 2:2]

These *wise* men, when they worshipped Christ, did not permit it to be a mere empty-handed adoration; and truly *wise* men are still liberal men.

C. H. Spurgeon, *Christ's Incarnation*, p. 104 [Matthew 2:2]

Wonder

Holy *wonder* will lead you to grateful worship.

C. H. Spurgeon, *Christ's Incarnation*, p. 37

There is more of God's glory and majesty to be seen in the manger and the cross than in the sparkling stars above, the rolling deep below, the towering mountain, the teeming valleys, the abodes of life, or the abyss of death. Let us then give ourselves up to holy *wonder*, such as will produce gratitude, worship, love, and confidence, as we think of that great "mystery of godliness, God manifest in the flesh."

C. H. Spurgeon, *Christ's Incarnation*, p. 38 [1 Timothy 3:16]

Word

The prayerful study of the *Word* is not only a means of instruction, but an act of devotion wherein the transforming power of grace is often exercised, changing us into the image of Him of whom the *Word* is a mirror.

The Greatest Fight in the World, C. H. Spurgeon's "Final Manifesto," p. 20 [2 Corinthians 3:18]

Is there anything, after all, like the *Word of God* when the open book finds open hearts? When I read the lives of such men as Baxter, Brainerd, M'Cheyne, and many others, why, I feel like one who has bathed himself in some cool brook after having gone a journey through a black country, which left him dusty and depressed; and this result comes of the fact that such men embodied *Scripture* in their lives and illustrated it in their experience. The washing of water by the *Word* is what they had and what we need.

The Greatest Fight in the World, C. H. Spurgeon's "Final Manifesto," p. 20

The *Bible*, brethren, is inexhaustible. A long life will only suffice us to skirt the shores of this great continent of light.

In the forty years of my own ministry I have only touched the hem of the garment of divine truth; but what virtue has flowed out of it! The *Word* is like its Author, infinite, immeasurable, without end. If you were ordained to be a preacher throughout eternity, you would have before you a theme equal to everlasting demands.

> *The Greatest Fight in the World,* C. H. Spurgeon's "Final Manifesto," p. 21

It is sadly common among ministers to add a word or subtract a word from the passage, or in some way to debase the language of *sacred writ*. Believers in verbal inspiration should be studiously careful to be verbally correct. Let us quote the *words as they stand in the best possible translation,* and it will be better still if we know the original, and can tell if our version fails to give the sense. How much mischief may arise out of an accidental alteration of the *Word!*

> *The Greatest Fight in the World,* C. H. Spurgeon's "Final Manifesto," p. 23

The *Word,* we say, is the only sword which the Spirit uses. I know the Holy Ghost uses gracious sermons; but it is only in proportion as they have the *Word of God* in them. I know the Holy Ghost uses religious books; but only so far as they are the *Word of God* told out in other language. Conviction, conversion, and consolation still are wrought, and only by the *Word of God.* . . . In contending against the powers of darkness, "The sword of the Spirit is the *Word of God.*" "It is written" is his master-stroke. *Words* which God has spoken by holy men of old, and has caused to be recorded on the sacred page—these are the battle-axe and weapons of war of his Spirit.

> C. H. Spurgeon, *Metropolitan Tabernacle Pulpit,* Vol. 37, p. 232 [Jude 3; Ephesians 6:17; James 3:17]

To become *"mighty in the Scriptures"* will be to become "mighty through God."

The Greatest Fight in the World, C. H. Spurgeon's "Final Manifesto," p. 24 [2 Corinthians 10:4–5]

Oh, for a mighty onslaught upon the powers of darkness! Once more, we are to take this sword with a purpose. We are to use it that we may be able to stand and to withstand. If you want to stand, draw the sword, and smite your doubts. How fiercely unbelief assails! Here comes a doubt as to your election. Pierce it through with the *Word*. Anon comes a doubt as to the precious blood. Cleave it from head to foot with the assurance of the Word that the blood of Jesus cleanseth us from all sin. Here comes another doubt, and yet another. As quick as arm can move, drive texts of *Scripture* through every new fallacy, every new denial of truth, and spit the whole of them upon the rapier of the *Word*. It will be for your good to kill these doubts outright. Do not play with them, but fight them in real earnest. You will find that temptations also will come in hordes. Meet them with the precepts of *sacred Writ*, and slay even the desire of evil by the Spirit's application of the *Holy Word*. The washing of water by the *Word* is a glorious cleanser. Discouragements will arise like mists of the morning. Oh, that *God's Word* may shine them away with the beams of the promises!

C. H. Spurgeon, *Metropolitan Tabernacle Pulpit*, Vol. 37, p. 239 [Ephesians 6:17; Jude 3; James 3:17]

Believe in the *inspired volume* up to the hilt. Believe it with the whole strength of your being. Let the truths of Scripture become the chief factors in your life, the chief operating forces of your action.

The Greatest Fight in the World, C. H. Spurgeon's "Final Manifesto," p. 24

We should resolve that we will quote more of *Holy Scripture*. Sermons should be full of *Bible;* sweetened, strengthened, sanctified with *Bible* essence. *Bible* hearers, when they hear indeed, come to be *Bible* lovers.

> *The Greatest Fight in the World,* C. H. Spurgeon's "Final Manifesto," p. 24

Our own words are mere paper pellets compared with the rifle shot of *the Word.*

> *The Greatest Fight in the World,* C. H. Spurgeon's "Final Manifesto," p. 24

It is glorious to be far out on the ocean of Divine love . . . steering for heaven straight away by the direction of the *Word* of God.

> C. H. Spurgeon, *Pearls From Many Seas,* Compiled by Rev. J. B. McClure, p. 179

Spurgeon found himself living with *God's Word* and its interpreters. Anything and everything that made God clear to the heart was relevant to Charles Spurgeon.

> Preface, *Devotions and Prayers of Charles H. Spurgeon*

His *Word* is a matchless temple where we delight to be, to contemplate the beauty.

> C. H. Spurgeon

You may have knowledge in the brain, but it may not run into your spirit, so as to penetrate, and permeate, and saturate your spirit, till you are filled therewith. Oh, to get the *Gospel* into one's entire nature, and to be like the waterpots of Cana, filled up to the brim! . . . Dive into the deeps and climb up to the heights, and . . . ask the Holy Spirit to saturate you with Truth, as Gideon's fleece was wet with the dew of heaven.

> C. H. Spurgeon, *The Treasury of David* [Colossians 3:16]

159

Hereby our growth in grace may be ascertained. Is *God's Word* very sweet to me this day?

> C. H. Spurgeon, *The Treasury of the Bible*, Vol. 3, p. 72 [Psalm 119:103]

"Order my steps in Thy *Word:* and let not any iniquity have dominion over me." You, too, who are just beginning to seek the Savior, should be told that this is the kind of spirit to which you will have to come; and if the Lord brings you to be His own, this is the kind of prayer that you will pray; and if you cannot pray it, and will not pray it, you will bear witness against yourselves that you are not the children of God.

> C. H. Spurgeon, *The Treasury of the Bible*, Vol. 3, p. 79 [Psalm 119:133]

Unless we do have deep awe of the *Word* we shall never have high joy over it. Our rejoicing will be measured by our reverencing.

> C. H. Spurgeon, *The Treasury of the Bible*, Vol. 3, p. 82 [Psalm 119:162]

The chief means of a man's revealing himself is by his word: language is the gate of the soul. If the man be true and honest, his word will be a window through which you may see his mind. . . . This written *Word* is the revelation of God, and when the Spirit of God shines upon it, we herein see the Lord as in a mirror.

> C. H. Spurgeon, *The Treasury of the Bible*, Vol. 3, p. 83 [Psalm 119:162; 2 Corinthians 3:18]

As the mariner prizes his chart and compass, so do we welcome the *Law of the Lord.* Tossed on the changing sea of life our eye is gladdened by the clear ray of this pole-star of heaven, the fixed light of God.

> C. H. Spurgeon, *The Treasury of the Bible*, Vol. 3, p. 83 [Psalm 119:162]

Seek to let the *Word* photograph itself upon your understanding, and then straight way when you know the divine will labour to carry it out in all particulars.

> C. H. Spurgeon, *The Treasury of the Bible,* Vol. 3, p. 36 [Psalm 119:6]

Heart-fellowship with God is enjoyed through a love of that *Word* which is God's way of communing with the soul by His Holy Spirit. Prayer and praise and all sorts of devotional acts and feelings gleam through the verses like beams of sunlight through an olive grove. You are not only instructed, but influenced to holy emotion, and helped to express the same.

> C. H. Spurgeon, *The Treasury of David,* Vol. 3, p. 139

It must . . . be our plan to keep the *Word* of the Lord much upon our minds; . . . only by daily communion with the Lord by *His Word* can we hope to learn His way, to be purged from defilement, and to be made to walk in His statutes.

> C. H. Spurgeon, *The Treasury of David,* Vol. 3, p. 141

Whenever a passage of *Scripture* sings to you of itself, sing with it before the Lord: whenever in reading, the verse seems to leap out of the page into your bosom, there let it lodge for ever.

> C. H. Spurgeon, *The Treasury of the Bible,* Vol. 3, p. 86 [Psalm 119:162]

This is the mark of the man who is taught of God,—that the *Word* is sweet to his mouth when he preaches it to others, as well as sweet to his taste when he meditates upon it himself.

> C. H. Spurgeon, *Spurgeon's Expository Encyclopedia,* Vol. 15, p. 266 [Psalm 119:103]

There is a joy arising out of the very fact that *Holy Scripture* may be considered to be a spoil.

> C. H. Spurgeon, *The Treasury of the Bible*, Vol. 3, p. 86 [Psalm 119:162]

As one has well said,—Here is the best thing,—"Thy Word"; hidden in the best place,—"in my heart"; for the best of purposes,—"that I might not sin against Thee."

> C. H. Spurgeon, *The Treasury of the Bible*, Vol. 3, p. 159 [Psalm 119:11]

He who intelligently and intensely knows the *Word* is likely to hold it fast.

> C. H. Spurgeon, *Spurgeon's Expository Encyclopedia*, Vol. 15, p. 396 [2 Samuel 23:9–10]

Scripture is . . . a rock of diamonds; it is a sacred collyrium, or eye-salve; it mends their eyes that look upon it; it is a spiritual optic-glass in which the glory of God is resplendent.

> C. H. Spurgeon, *The Treasury of David*, Vol. 3, p. 285 [Psalm 119:72]

Work

God buries the workman, but the devil himself cannot bury the *work*. The *work* is everlasting, though the workmen die.

> C. H. Spurgeon, *We Endeavour*, p. 81

World

How gloriously doth sacred joy lift us up above the sorrows of the *world!* Yea, more, how it lifts us up above earth's joys! The man who has once drunk the old wine of the kingdom does not desire the new and sour wine of earth.

> C. H. Spurgeon, *Spurgeon's Expository Encyclopedia*, Vol. 10, p. 61 [Isaiah 61:3; 1 John 1:1–4; Romans 15:13]

Worship

Our Father, which art in heaven, hallowed be Thy name.
. . . With heart and mind, and memory and fear, and hope
and joy, we worship the Most High. . . . With lowliest reverence, with truest love, we worship God in Christ Jesus, uniting therewith with all the redeemed host above, with angels
and principalities and powers.

> C. H. Spurgeon, *C. H. Spurgeon's Prayers*, p. 67 [Matthew
> 6:9]

Wrath of God

The preaching of the *wrath of God* has come to be sneered
at nowadays, and even good people are half-ashamed of it;
a maudlin sentimentality about love and goodness has
hushed, in great measure, plain gospel expostulations and
warnings. But, if we expect souls to be saved, we must declare unflinchingly with all affectionate fidelity, the *terrors*
of the Lord.

> C. H. Spurgeon, *Words of Counsel for Christian Workers*, p. 15
> [2 Corinthians 5:11]

Zeal

Believe me, brethren and sisters, if you never have sleep-
less hours, if you never have weeping eyes, if your hearts
never swell as if they would burst, you need not anticipate
that you will be called *zealous;* you do not know the beginning of true *zeal,* for the foundation of Christian *zeal* lies in
the heart. The heart must be heavy with grief and yet must
beat high with holy ardour; the heart must be vehement in
desire, panting continually for God's glory. . . . *Zeal* mani-
fests itself, let me say that it is always seen, where it is gen-

uine, in a vehement love and attachment to the person of the
Saviour.

C. H. Spurgeon, *Spurgeon's Expository Encyclopedia*, Vol. 15,
p. 421 [Luke 6:15]

Oh! God of *zeal*, drop thy *zeal* upon us now, and make us
zealous too, even we, by blood redeemed, by Thy Holy
Spirit, inhabit, consecrate us afresh, for Jesus' sake. Amen.

C. H. Spurgeon, *Spurgeon's Expository Encyclopedia*, Vol. 15,
p. 389 [Isaiah 9:7]

We judge of a man's *zeal* when the purpose has been long
in his heart, and he has most industriously followed it
through a long period.

C. H. Spurgeon, *Spurgeon's Expository Encyclopedia*, Vol. 15,
p. 389 [Isaiah 9:7]

When the Christian church *glows* in this fashion, it will
swell with an intense heat like a volcano, whose tremendous
furnaces cannot be contained within itself, but its sides begin to move and bulge, and then after a rumbling and a
heaving, a mighty sheet of fire shoots right up to heaven, and
afterwards streams of flaming lava run from its red lips
down, burning their way along the plain beneath. Oh! to get
such a fire for God's cause into the heart of the Christian
church, till she begins to heave and throb with unquench-
able emotion, and then a mighty sheet of the fire-prayer
should go up towards Heaven, and afterwards the burning
lava of her all-conquering *zeal* should flow over all lands,
till all nations should enquire: "What is this new thing in
the earth, and what this modern miracle, and what this cross
of Christ for which men live and die?"

C. H. Spurgeon, *Spurgeon's Expository Encyclopedia*, Vol. 15,
p. 316 [Acts 2:17]

Oh! God, where, where, where is Thy *zeal?* . . . Hast Thou
forgotten Thy Son, His griefs, His merits; Thy promised rec-

ompense to Him? Where is Thy *zeal?* Oh! but this is a battering ram with which to shake the very gates of Heaven. Men of prayer and faith, learn how to use this!

C. H. Spurgeon, *Spurgeon's Expository Encyclopedia*, Vol. 15, p. 387 [Isaiah 9:7]

Zeal is essential to success; we only wish that Christians would take copy from worldly men and be half as earnest and half as ambitious to maintain and increase the kingdom of their Lord and Master, as some men are after petty trifles or selfish aggrandisements.

C. H. Spurgeon, *Spurgeon's Expository Encyclopedia*, Vol. 15, p. 414 [Luke 6:15]

Look at Saul of Tarsus; no man more *zealous* against the gospel than he, and he is second to none when he becomes a preacher of the Word.

C. H. Spurgeon, *Spurgeon's Expository Encyclopedia*, Vol. 15, p. 418 [Luke 6:15]

On the "Down-Grade," the train travels fast. . . . A craven spirit is upon many, and their tongues are paralyzed. Oh, for an outburst of true faith and holy *zeal!*

C. H. Spurgeon, *The "Down-Grade" Controversy*, p. 76 [Revelation 3:19]

Appendix **A**

God's Terms of Salvation

What is it to believe in Him? It is not merely to say, "He is God and the Saviour," but to trust Him wholly and entirely, and take Him for all your salvation from this time forth and forever—your *Lord*, your *Master*, your *All*.

C. H. Spurgeon, *All of Grace*, pp. 30–31

If any man would be saved, he must believe that Jesus Christ is both *Lord* and *God*. Again, you must confess that Jesus Christ is *Lord*, that is, *Ruler* and *Master*. You must cheerfully become His disciple, follower, and servant. You must confess, "He is my *Master*; He is my *Lord*. I intend to be a soldier under Him. He shall be to me *Leader* and *Commander;* God has made Him such, and I accept Him as such." You are vocally to own Jesus; you are definitely and distinctly to say with your tongue, your mouth, your lips, that He is your *Lord* and *Saviour*. . . .

With my mouth I do again confess the Lord Jesus, for I believe Him to be *very God of very God,* my *Master,* my *All.*

> C. H. Spurgeon, *Metropolitan Tabernacle Pulpit,* Vol. 32,
> pp. 247–248, 252 [Romans 10:9]

Do not imagine that the Gospel is magnified or God glorified by going to worldlings and telling them that they may be saved at this moment simply by accepting Christ as their Saviour while they're wedded to their idols and their hearts are still in love with sin. If I do so, I tell them a lie, I pervert the gospel, I insult Christ and turn the grace of God into lasciviousness.

> C. H. Spurgeon

Submission to the will of God, to Christ's lordship, and to the guiding of the Spirit is an essential, not an optional, part of *saving faith.* A new, untaught believer will understand little of the full implications of such obedience, but the spiritual orientation of his new nature in Christ will bring a desire for submission to God's Word and God's Spirit. A person who does not have that desire has no legitimate claim on *salvation.*

> John MacArthur, *The MacArthur New Testament Commentary*
> (Ephesians), p. 249 [Ephesians 5:18b–21]

A defective theology . . . has crept over us like a deadening fog. This theology separates faith from discipleship and grace from obedience. It teaches that Jesus can be received as one's Saviour without being received as one's Lord. . . . In these times, preachers often delude them with an *"easy" faith*—Christianity without the cross—in order to increase the numbers on their church rolls, whether or not the added people are regenerate.

Dietrich Bonhoeffer, the German churchman of the Nazi era who eventually suffered martyrdom for his opposition to Hitler's policies, called this erroneous theology *"cheap grace."* . . . *Cheap grace* is grace without discipleship, grace without the cross.

> James Montgomery Boice, *Christ's Call to Discipleship,* p. 14

"Not everyone that saith unto me, Lord, Lord, shall enter into the kingdom of heaven; but he that *doeth the will of my Father* which is in heaven" (Matthew 7:21). This is New Testament Christianity. Scripture speaks about *holiness* without which no man shall see the Lord. "Blessed are the *pure in heart,* for they (and nobody else) shall see God."

But a very subtle danger arises at this point, and I have no doubt the Apostle had it in mind when he wrote the very words we are considering. There are people who will argue, "But wait a minute; are you not preaching the law to us? . . . Surely you are forgetting the gospel! You have been referring to the original kingdom, and the original law that God held before mankind; but now the Lord Jesus Christ has come, and we are confronted by something quite new; we are no longer confronted by the demands of the law and the tremendous holiness of God. It is just a matter of believing on the Lord Jesus Christ, and we shall be saved." Now that is their argument, but I am bound to say that it is one of the most subtle, dangerous heresies that can ever be offered to men and women. And yet it characterizes a great deal of modern evangelism. . . . *"God is made unto us wisdom, and righteousness, and sanctification, and redemption!"* There is the whole process. And the truth is, that if you are in it at all, you are in it at every point. . . . The God who justifies goes on with the process. And unless we are giving evidence of being in the process . . . there is but one conclusion to draw—we have never been in the kingdom at all.

> D. Martyn Lloyd-Jones, *Darkness and Light: An Exposition of Ephesians 4:17–5:17,* pp. 346–353 [Matthew 5:8; Hebrews 12:14]

Nowadays we have created an artificial distinction between trusting Christ as Saviour and confessing Him as Lord. We have made two experiences out of it when it is one. So we have a host who have "accepted Christ" in order to miss hell and reach heaven, who seem not at all concerned about making Him *Lord* of their lives. Salvation is not a cafeteria line where we can take the Saviourhood of Christ and pass up His Lordship, take what we want and leave the rest. We cannot get saved on the installment plan, with fingers crossed and inner reservations, as though one could take Christ "on approval." To be sure, one may not understand all that is involved at conversion, but no man can knowingly and willfully take Christ as Saviour and reject Him as Lord, and be saved. Paul told the Philippian jailer, "Believe on the Lord Jesus Christ and thou shalt be saved." He presented all three names of our Lord as Master, Mediator and Messiah. He would not have the jailer take Christ as Saviour and think over His Lordship until some later time.

We have only one option: we can receive the Lord or reject Him. But once we receive Him our option ends. We are then no longer our own but

169

bought with a price. We belong to Him. He has the first word and the last. He demands absolute loyalty beyond that of any earthly dictator but He has a right to do it. "Love so amazing, so divine, demands my soul, my life, my all."

There is a *cheap, easy believism* that does not believe and a receivism that does not receive. There is no real confession of Jesus as Lord. It is significant that the word "Saviour" occurs only twenty-four times in the New Testament, while the word "Lord" is found 433 times. A Christian is a believer, a disciple and a witness.

> Vance Havner, *The Best of Vance Havner*, pp. 124–126 [Acts 16:31; 2 Corinthians 4:5]

The baby *sucks*, instinctively; and the born-again person also feels a hunger for spiritual food—first the milk and then the meat of God's revealed Word (1 Peter 2:2; Hebrews 5:12–14; 1 Corinthians 3:2). He listens to the Word preached and taught and discussed; he reads it in his Bible, and in books that throw light on the Bible; he asks questions about it; he meditates on it, memorizes it, chews the cud on it, labours to squeeze all the goodness out of it. "Oh, how I love Thy law! It is my meditation all the day . . . How sweet are Thy words to my taste, sweeter than honey to my mouth!" (Psalm 119:97, 103). Constantly to crave for God's Word and to want to go deeper into it is thus a second sign of being regenerate. . . . Regeneration is no more (and no less!) than the work of God in our hearts which leads to *the gospel* being whole-heartedly received. If only God would make us simple enough to see this and, having seen it, never to lose sight of it! Then the Christian world would be a very different place.

> J. I. Packer, *God's Words*, pp. 154–155 [Romans 6:17]

Appendix B

Prayers and Paraphrased Prayers of Charles Spurgeon, Scripture, and Others

Approximately 50 percent of the prayers in this appendix are Charles Spurgeon's. The rest are by the compiler or John H. Jowett, George Morrison, Alexander Maclaren, F. B. Meyer, John F. MacArthur, Jr., A. W. Tozer, Thomas Manton, Joseph Parker, Joseph Alleine, Count Zinzendorf, and unknown Puritans.

* 1. O God and Father of our Lord Jesus Christ, by Thy Holy Spirit, give us eyes to see the excellencies of Jesus, and then, to exchange all that we are for all that Christ is! [Psalm 84:9. See also "Substitution," pp. 137–139]

2. Give us the grace to take Thy holiness for our happiness.

3. Make our praises equal to our expectations and our expectations equal to Thy promises.

4. Glorify Thy Son that Thy Son may also glorify Thee. [John 17:1]

5. Accept these our poor praises.

6. If we think that we love Thee more than we do, we pray that we may yet love Thee more than we think.

7. May Thy pardoned ones have a renewed sense of their acceptance in the Beloved.

8. Keep us true in doctrine, true in experience, true in life, true in word, true in deed.

9. Let those whom you gave to Christ be brought out from among the ruins of the fall to be His joy and crown.

10. We thank Thee for the manifestation of Him even in the types and shadows of the Old Testament.

11. Bless Thy people by saturating them with [in] the Word of Thy truth.

12. Shine upon us, O Lord, that we may reflect Thy brightness.

13. Elevate us into Thy presence, and in all circumstances glorify Thyself in and through us.

14. How we need the clear shinings of Thy love, the beams of Thy grace, the light of Thy countenance.

15. Lord, extend the kingdom of Thy dear Son.

16. Tune our lips to the melody of thanksgiving.

17. Help us to mingle our feeble prayers with the intercessions of our Great High Priest.

18. Help us to realize more and more that we live and move and have our being in Thee.

19. Be within us a light that does not dazzle, a fire that does not consume.

20. Do Thou lift us up again into the sunlight of Thy forgiveness.

21. Dry the tears of unusual sorrow.

22. May we live in daily anticipation of the manifestations of Thy love. Lord, continually remind me that You are right beside me.

23. Dear Saviour, do Thou be mine and I will be Thine.

24. O my spotless, fairest Beloved: I would ever be with Thee.

25. O my blessed Master, help me I pray Thee to keep the mirror of my mind in the right position, that evermore I may see Thee.

26. Let me count that gain to be loss which is gained by loss of communion with Thee.

27. Help us, O Lord, to believe in Thee with childlike faith when clouds and darkness hide Thy throne.

28. How we praise Thee, O Lord, that Christ's great passion is to love and lift our fragmentary lives till they are brought into the image of His own.

29. How we praise Thee, O Lord, that Christ was a master swordsman with the sword of the Spirit at the very outset of His ministry.

30. O Lord, may the energy of Thy divine affection roll abundantly to the shores of human need.

31. O Holy Spirit, as the sun is full of light, the ocean full of water, Heaven full of glory, so may my heart be full of Thee. Give me Thyself without measure as an unimpaired fountain, as inexhaustible riches.

32. Great God, we long that false doctrine may fly like birds of darkness before the light of Thy coming.

33. We do with all our hearts pray, "Thy kingdom come, Thy will be done on earth, as it is in heaven." Lord, help us to do Thy will. Take the crippled kingdom of our manhood and reign Thou over it. Sit Thou on the glorious high throne in our hearts, and may our lives prove that Thou art Lord over us; by our every thought and desire, and imagination, and word, and act, in every respect being under Thy divine control.

34. Let me find Thy light in my darkness, Thy life in my death, Thy joy in my sorrow, Thy grace in my sin, Thy riches in my poverty, Thy glory in my valley.

35. My Father, magnify Thy love to me according to its greatness, and not according to my deserts or prayers, and whatever increase Thou givest, let it draw out greater love to Thee.

36. Grant us the grace to give Thee full opportunity to manifest Thy glory.

37. It is heaven on earth to feel Thine eye upon us and know that it is love.

38. O my Saviour, ever lift us up to stand and walk with Thee on the high level of Thy manifested presence and glory.

39. Father, we would worship Thee. May all that we are react rightly to all that Thou art.

40. O our Father, for the purpose of manifesting Thy glory in the most marvelous way, may our salvation indeed be a gradual but assured ascension into the strength and beauty of the King.

41. King of glory, we are poor and needy—bless us with the unsearchable riches of Christ.

42. Merciful Father, I humbly ask that the Holy Spirit may open my eyes more fully to behold and my heart more ardently to love Thee in Him, Who is the brightness of Thy glory, the express image of Thy person.

43. O God of truth, help me to distill from Thy Word faithful, effectual, fervent prayer.

44. O my Lord, cause me and all Thy people to behold Thee—here in the light of special faith and hereafter in the blaze of endless glory.

45. O my Saviour, grind to dust the evil heart of unbelief. Make it my chiefest joy to study Thee, meditate on Thee, gaze on Thee.

46. O Lord, let us gaze upon Thy glory till we are transformed by the sight and become Christlike among the sons of men.

47. Grant us a faith, O God, that enables us so to rejoice in Thee, that our infirmities become platforms for the display of Thy grace.

48. O God, we praise Thee for the divine blessing that has come streaming down to us through each one of those condescending titles worn by the Father, Son and Holy Spirit.

* 49. Father, may the roots of Thine own go down deep into the soil of Thy marvelous love. [Ephesians 3:17—*The Living Bible*]

50. O Love irresistible, come forth and carry by blessed storm, the hearts that have not yet yielded to Thee.

51. O Father of Jesus, let the mighty tide of His everlasting love cover the rocks of my sin and care.

52. Sovereign Lord, possess our minds with the grandeur of Thy perfections.

53. I am unworthy, O Lord, everlastingly unworthy to be Thine.

54. O blessed Trinity: O glorious Unity! I deliver myself up to Thee.

55. Dwell in us, O Jesus, that out of us may come the power of Thy life.

56. O blessed hand of Jesus, drive in the nail of Divine love.

57. Lord, throw down the Jezebel of our unbelief and let the dogs devour it.

58. O Lord, we would dwell in Thy secret place, abiding under the shadow of the Almighty. [Psalm 91:1]

59. Tune my nature that my life may make music to Thy praise.

60. Be more real to our apprehensions and thus more fully master of our affections.

61. May our souls know their hunger and be able to express it in earnest, urgent prayer.

62. We leave this poor prayer at Thy footstool, for surely Thy grace will turn it into a great answer.

63. Almighty God, may we by faith lay hold of Thy words of love.

64. Allow us to behold Jesus in all the wondrousness of His beauty and holiness.

65. We praise Thee for Thy veiled grace even in Thy afflicting providence.

66. How we praise Thee, our Father, that our infirmities become the black velvet on which the diamond of Thy love glitters all the more brightly.

67. Father, may praise be the alpha and omega of our Christian life.

68. May praise be the very life of our life.

69. How we thank Thee that praise is the rehearsal of our eternal song.

70. Give us the grace to realize that an infinite reservoir of power is waiting to be tapped by the hand of faith.

71. How we praise Thee that the resurrection is an ongoing thing.

72. Grant us the power of strenuous, studious prayer.

73. May our praise be a rhapsody of love in the presence of our Beloved.

74. Tune my heart to sing Thy praise.

75. May the glory of Thy grace strike the chords of our hearts into music, so that our life resounds with exuberant praise.

76. Help our souls to catch glimpses of the riches of His grace till the wonder of the vision moves us to inevitable and immediate praise.

77. Lord, grant us that brand of praise which is filled with exhilarating gratitude which springs from sacred joy.

78. O Father, unseal rivers of energy and direct them to the crying needs of the universe.

79. Father, great triune God, we desire to love Thee infinitely and please Thee infinitely and bring Thee infinite joy.

80. Father, the joy of our joy is to bring joy to the heart of Christ.

81. Father, how we praise Thee for the matchless condescension of Christ!—from the infinity of God to the weakness of a thirsting, dying man.

82. How we praise Thee our Father, that from Old Testament times right up to the present, Thy prophets always brought with them a light brighter than the twilight of accepted compromise.

83. God of all grace, may the ocean of Thy grace flow about the shore of common life into all its distresses and gaping wants.

84. Father of mercies, tenderly take to Thy loving heart, each and every one of Thy departing saints, that at last they may be where Christ is—gazing on His glory and thus fulfilling His heart's desire. [John 17:24]

85. Father, give us the grace to leave our usefulness to Thee to estimate. May we trust Thee fully to see to it that we do not live our lives in vain, but rather bring much glory to Thee.

86. Lord, how we praise Thee for those of Thy saints who for love of Thee and Thy cause, have put forth strenuous effort habitually and spurts of energy up to the very edge of human endurance. May we by Thy grace seek to follow these as they followed Christ.

87. Great triune God, King of Kings, how we praise Thee for Thy incomprehensible condescension wherein you veil your sovereignty and stoop to beseeching Thy creatures to receive the love You offer and be reconciled to Thee! [2 Corinthians 5:20—*The Living Bible*]

88. Help us, O our Father, by Thy spirit to be cheerful, sacrificial givers in our intercessions, fellow-laborers along with the Lord Jesus Christ, that the holy, invincible powers of Thy grace may be distributed over a desperately needy multitude.

89. How we praise Thee, Lord Jesus, that You were ever leading the woman at the well upward—from the well of Jacob to the well springs that are found in Jacob's God.

For Thy name's sake, may this be the experience of countless multitudes among the lost.

90. Help us to realize, our Father, that we conquer—not in any brilliant fashion, but rather, we conquer by continuing.

91. Lord of Hosts, how we long to be with Thee, where we too may live and love in the undivided eternity, above the low fences of time.

92. Father, help us not to be impatient for Thee to act. Rather, give us the grace to keep traveling steadily along Thy pathway that in due season You may honor us with every blessing. [Psalm 37:34—*The Living Bible*]

93. We pray, Father, that all Thy people might be filled with Thy mighty, glorious strength so that they can keep going no matter what happens, always full of Thy joy. [Colossians 1:11—*The Living Bible*]

* 94. Lord Jesus, shout in the ear of Satan that You exposed him and all the demons to be shattered, empty and defeated in Thy own triumphant victory at the cross where You shed Thy precious blood for the sin of the world. [Colossians 2:15—Phillips]

* 95. Father, give us the grace right now to consider ourselves dead indeed unto sin but alive unto Thee through Jesus Christ our Lord. Let this be true for all Thy people. [Romans 6:11]

96. O Divine Master, may we ever come to Thee with empty hands to receive whatever Thy grace and mercy is willing to bestow upon us in Christ.

97. Please, O Lord, ever grant us that faith that unfolds the eternal in the moment, the infinite in the trifle, the divine in the commonplace.

98. How we praise Thee, our Father, that faith hath wings and meditation is its chariot.

99. Grant us, O Father, we pray, great faith, because we know that faith is the grace that brings most glory to Thee.

100. Shine in Thou light of life, and make my soul the radiant witness of Thy grace.

101. May Thy beauty, O Lord our God, be upon us. [Psalm 90:17]

102. How we praise Thee O God that Thy pure, full love streams through the *blood* and *obedience* of Jesus to every soul lying under them, however vile and wretched in themselves.

103. Lord, how we praise Thee that even our tears are made to glisten in the radiant light of faith and hope.

104. Father, help us ever to be filled with the fruits of righteousness, which are by Jesus Christ, unto Thy glory and praise. [Philippians 1:11]

105. Father, we praise Thee that you are able to make all grace abound toward us; that we, always having all sufficiency in all things, may abound to every good work. [2 Corinthians 9:8]

106. Father, ever enable us by Thy Holy Spirit, to take Thy precious Word as the very sword of the Spirit that it truly is—for though we walk in the flesh, we do not war according to the flesh: (for the weapons of our warfare are not carnal, but mighty through Thee to the pulling down of strongholds;) casting down imaginations, and every high thing that exalts itself against the knowledge of Thee and bringing into captivity every thought to the obedience of Christ. [Ephesians 6:17; 2 Corinthians 10:3–5]

107. Ah, Lord! Square me till I am fit for a place in Thy temple; prune me till I yield my utmost fruit. I know not what this prayer may involve; but if I did, I would pray to be helped to pray it, and I would entreat Thee to fulfill it to the letter.

* 108. Father, may the power of Thy blessed Holy Spirit working through us, accomplish infinitely more for the cause of Christ than we could ever ask or imagine. [Ephesians 3:20—*The Living Bible*]

Prayer to Receive Christ

Lord Jesus, as best I know how, I am coming to You, admitting that I am a lost sinner, and asking You to come into my life and save me and change me, and make me the kind of person You want me to be.

Give me the grace (or ability) to trust You and You alone, Lord Jesus, for this salvation and this change You bring. In Your name I pray, Lord Jesus. Amen.

Breath—Heartbeat Prayer to Receive Christ (For those who lack the assurance of salvation.)

Lord Jesus, if there is any chance that I am not now saved, let every breath that I breathe, and every heartbeat that my heart beats, call upon You, asking You to come into my life and save me and change me, and make me the kind of person You want me to be. Give me the grace (or ability) to trust You and You alone, Lord Jesus, from this moment on, for this salvation and the change You bring. In Your name I pray, Lord Jesus. Amen.

Compiler pleads with fellow Christians to make numbers. 1, 49, 94, 95, and 108 a part of their daily private life, and in general, to PRAY THE WORD MUCH!

Conformed to Christ
(2 Corinthians 3:18; John 17:24)

Our salvation is a gradual, but assured ascension into the strength and beauty of the King.

> John H. Jowett, *Epistles of St. Peter*, p. 33

His great passion is to love and lift our fragmentary lives till they are brought into the image of His own.

> George H. Morrison, *The Footsteps of the Flock*, p. 96
> [Matthew 14:13–21]

Seek to live with such lucidity that the clarity of your motives becomes a lens which projects the image of Christ upon the screens of others' lives.

> David Augsburger, *Witness Is Withness*, p. 60

There is a slow but steady *transmutation* of the base metal of human nature into the gold of Godlikeness effected by the faith-filled *gaze* of the soul at the *glory* of God in the face of Jesus Christ.

A. W. Tozer

God . . . hath shined in our hearts that we might *reflect* to others the light of the knowledge of the glory of God in the face of Jesus Christ.

Alexander Maclaren

You can take nothing greater to the heathen world than the impress and *reflection* of the love of God upon your own character.

Henry Drummond

Beholding the *glory* of Christ in the blessed glass of the Gospel, we are changed into the same image and likeness by the Spirit of the Lord. . . . *Faith* is the *light* wherein we *behold* the *glory of Christ* in this world.

John Owen, *The Glory of Christ*, pp. 186–187

For if our future blessedness shall consist in being where He is and *beholding His glory*, what better preparation can there be for it than a constant previous contemplation of that *glory* as revealed in the Gospel, that . . . we may be gradually transformed into the same *glory?*

John Owen, *The Glory of Christ* (back cover)

Conformity

Oh, to be like Thee, dear Jesus, my plea,
Just to know Thou art formed fully in me.
On with Thy beauty, Lord, off with my sin,
Fixed on Thy glory Thy likeness to win.

Oh, to be like Thee, Thine image display,
This is the Spirit's work day after day.
Glory to glory transformed by His grace,
Till in Thy presence I stand face to face.

Oh, to be like Thee, Thou lover of men,
Gracious and gentle compassionate friend.
Merciful Saviour, such kindness and care,
Are only mine when Thy likeness I share.

To be like Thee, Jesus!
To be like Thee, Jesus!
For this I live; to this I'll die;
It is my hope, my prayer, my cry.

John F. MacArthur, Jr., *Keys to Spiritual Growth*

Appendix D

Alexander Maclaren (of Wife)

In 1856 Marion McLaren became my wife. God allowed us to be together till the dark December of 1884. Others could speak of her charm, her beauty, her gifts and goodness. Most of what she was to me is for ever locked in my heart. But I would fain that, in any notices of what I am, or have been able to do, it should be told that the best part of it all came and comes from her. We read and thought together, and her clear, bright intellect illumined obscurities and "rejoiced in the truth." We worked and bore together, and her courage and deftness made toil easy and charmed away difficulties. She lived a life of nobleness, of strenuous effort, of aspiration, of sympathy, self-forgetfulness, and love. She was my guide, my inspirer, my corrector, my reward. Of all human formative influences on my character and life hers is the strongest and the best. To write of me and not to name her is to present a fragment.

Alexander Maclaren, *Exposition of Holy Scripture*, Vol. 17, Pt. 2, p. vii, *An Appreciation by W. Robertson Nicoll* [Proverbs 31]

Notes

Introduction

1. *The Soul Winner,* p. 312.

2. See "Supplication."

3. *Lectures to My Students,* p. 342.

4. See compiler's comment after first quote under "Conformed to Christ"; also Appendix C. [John 17:24; 2 Corinthians 3:18 Amplified Bible].

5. *Metropolitan Tabernacle Pulpit,* Vol. 27, p. 42.

6. *The Greatest Fight in the World,* C. H. Spurgeon's "Final Manifesto," p. 19.

7. Ibid., p. 23

8. See third quote under the heading "Holy Spirit," especially compiler's paraphrase.

Bibliography

The following books by Charles H. Spurgeon were used in compiling the quotes contained in this book.

Able to the Uttermost, Pilgrim Publications, Pasadena, TX, 1985.

According to Promise, Baker Book House, Grand Rapids, MI, 1980.

All of Grace, Baker Book House, Grand Rapids, MI, 1976.

An All-Round Ministry, The Banner of Truth Trust, Carlisle, PA, 1978.

Barbed Arrows, Christian Publications, Inc., Harrisburg, PA, 1970.

The Best of C. H. Spurgeon, Baker Book House, Grand Rapids, MI, 1979.

The Bible and the Newspaper, Pilgrim Publications, Pasadena, TX, 1973.

The Clue of the Maze, Pilgrim Publications, Pasadena, TX, (Reprinted from Passmore & Alabaster 1892 Edition).

C. H. Spurgeon Autobiography: 1, The Early Years, The Banner of Truth Trust, Carlisle, PA, 1981.

C. H. Spurgeon's Prayers, Baker Book House, Grand Rapids, MI, 1981.

Christ's Glorious Achievements, Baker Book House, Grand Rapids, MI, 1981.

Bibliography

Christ's Incarnation, Pilgrim Publications, Pasadena, TX, 1978.

Come Ye Children, Pilgrim Publications, Pasadena, TX, 1975.

Complete in Christ and Love's Logic, Baker Book House, Grand Rapids, MI, 1978.

Day by Day, Word Incorporated, Waco, TX, 1985.

Devotions and Prayers of Charles H. Spurgeon, Baker Book House, Grand Rapids, MI, 1976.

The "Down-Grade" Controversy, Pilgrim Publications, Pasadena, TX, 1978.

Eccentric Preachers, Pilgrim Publications, Pasadena, TX, 1978.

Faith's Checkbook, Moody Press, Chicago, IL, 1987.

Flowers From a Puritan's Garden, Sprinkle Publications, Harrisburg, VA, 1976.

Gleanings Among the Sheaves, Baker Book House, Grand Rapids, MI, 1977.

The Greatest Fight in the World, Pilgrim Publications, Pasadena, TX, 1990.

John Ploughman's Talks, Baker Book House, Grand Rapids, MI, 1982.

Lectures to My Students, Zondervan Publishing House, Grand Rapids, MI, 1970.

Memories of Stambourne, Pilgrim Publications, Pasadena, TX, 1974.

Metropolitan Tabernacle Pulpit, Vols. 26 (1880) through 31 (1885), The Banner of Truth Trust, Carlisle, PA, 1971.

Ibid., Vols. 32 (1886) and 33 (1887), 1969.

Ibid., Vols. 34 (1888) through 37 (1891), 1970.

Morning and Evening, Macdonald Publ. Co., Mclean, VA, n.d.

My Sermon Notes, Vol. 4, Baker Book House, Grand Rapids, MI, 1983.

The New Park Street Pulpit, Vols. 1, 2, and 4, Pilgrim Publications, Pasadena, TX, 1981.

Sermons in Candles, Baker Book House, Grand Rapids, MI, 1978.

Seven Wonders of Grace, Baker Book House, Grand Rapids, MI, 1979.

The Soul Winner, Wm. B. Eerdmans Publishing Co., Grand Rapids, MI, 1976.

Speeches at Home and Abroad, Pilgrim Publications, Pasadena, TX, 1974.

Spurgeon's Expository Encyclopedia, Vols. 7, 8, 10, and 15, Baker Book House, Grand Rapids, MI, 1984.

Spurgeon's Sermons Preached on Unusual Occasions, Pilgrim Publications, Pasadena, TX, 1978.

12 Sermons on the Resurrection, Baker Book House, Grand Rapids, MI, 1972.

Teachings of Nature in the Kingdom of Grace, Pilgrim Publications, Pasadena, TX, 1975.

The Treasury of C. H. Spurgeon, Baker Book House, Grand Rapids, MI, 1970.

The Treasury of David, Vol. 1, Zondervan Publishing House, Grand Rapids, MI, 1969.

Ibid., Vols. 2 and 3, Zondervan Publishing House, Grand Rapids, MI, 1974.

The Treasury of the Bible, Vols. 3 through 8, Baker Book House, Grand Rapids, MI, 1981.

We Endeavour, Pilgrim Publications, Pasadena, TX, 1975.

What the Stones Say, or *Sermons in Stones*, Pilgrim Publications, Pasadena, TX, 1975.

Words of Cheer for Daily Life, Pilgrim Publications, Pasadena, TX, 1978.

Words of Counsel for Christian Workers, Pilgrim Publications, Pasadena, TX, 1985.

Words of Warning for Daily Life, Pilgrim Publications, Pasadena, TX, 1980.

Words of Warning for Daily Life, Pilgrim Publications, Pasadena, TX, 1979.

Other sources quoted:

Augsburger, David, *Witness Is Withness*, Moody Press, Chicago, IL, 1971.

Boice, James Montgomery, *Christ's Call to Discipleship*, Moody Press, Chicago, IL, 1986.

Day, Richard E., *The Shadow of the Broad Brim*, Baker Book House, Grand Rapids, MI, 1976.

Havner, Vance, *The Best of Vance Havner*, Baker Book House, Grand Rapids, MI, 1981.

Jowett, John H., *Epistles of St. Peter*, Kregel Publications, Grand Rapids, MI, 1970.

Bibliography

————, *The Preacher: His Life and Work* (Yale Lectures, 1911), Baker Book House, Grand Rapids, MI, 1969.

Lloyd-Jones, D. Martyn, *Preaching and Preachers*, Zondervan Publishing House, Grand Rapids, MI, 1973.

MacArthur, Jr., John, *Keys to Spiritual Growth*, Fleming H. Revell Co., Old Tappan, NJ, 1976.

————, *The MacArthur New Testament Commentary* (Matthew 1–7), Moody Press, Chicago, Il, 1985.

Maclaren, Alexander, *Christ in the Heart*, n.p., n.d.

————, *Expositions of Holy Scripture* (Vol. 17, Pt. 2), Baker Book House, Grand Rapids, MI, 1974.

Morgan, G. Campbell, *Preaching*, Baker Book House, Grand Rapids, MI, 1974.

Morrison, George H., *The Footsteps of the Flock*, Baker Book House, Grand Rapids, MI, 1977.

Murray, Iain H., *The Forgotten Spurgeon*, The Banner of Truth Trust, Carlisle, PA, 1978.

Owen, John, *The Glory of Christ*, Moody Press, Chicago, IL, 1980.

Packer, J. I., *God's Words*, InterVarsity Press, Downers Grove, IL, 1981.

Ross, Bob L., Compiler, *An Introduction to the Life and Ministry of Charles Haddon Spurgeon*, Pilgrim Publications, Pasadena, TX, n.d.

Sheehan, R. J., *C. H. Spurgeon and the Modern Church*, Grace Publ. Trust, London, England, 1985.

Topical Index

Topical Index

Scripture Index